David Wilkerson Speaks Out

David Wilkerson Speaks Out

bethany fellowship

Library of Congress Cataloging in Publication Data

Wilkerson, David R
David Wilkerson Speaks Out
1. Theology—Addresses, essays, lectures
I. Title
BR85.W566
241
73-17303
ISBN 0-87123-089-5
ISBN 0-87123-091-7 (pbk.)

Bethany Fellowship, Inc.
6820 Auto Club Road
Minneapolis, Minnesota 55438

Printed in the United States of America

Introduction

Speaking out is always costly. If you keep at it, nearly everyone is offended because you eventually get around to discussing everybody's sacred opinions. I know this is true. This book contains a number of my recent "Speak Out" articles dealing with some of the most important issues of today. When the first message appeared in a magazine, friends and supporters applauded me for my "courage" and begged me to continue speaking out on other issues. But month by month, fewer and fewer accolades came my way. Instead, critics began to appear from every corner of the nation.

Christians everywhere could agree with what I had to say about gossip, but they were completely divided on my thoughts about tongues, demons, and doctrinal issues. Many supporters dropped off, claiming I had no right to be involved in controversial issues and that I should stick to helping drug addicts. "Speaking Out" cost our organization thousands of dollars in support—it cost me the friendship of many friends —and it brought an avalanche of hate-mail. But it accomplished something worth more than all the negative reactions—and that was THE BRIDGING OF MANY GAPS and the healing of many polarized attitudes.

The most important reason I can think of for speaking out today is the critical hour in which we live. There are issues that must be faced head-on, and there are many voices clamoring to be heard. There is precious little time left to get our house in order. I decided, prayerfully, that with God's help I would never again waste an opportunity to speak out fearlessly on those issues that most affected my life and ministry. Not for the sake of being controversial, but for the sake of being honest with myself.

To my way of thinking, there is nothing spectacular or new in this book, and some of my thoughts may completely miss the mark. But I can tell you as honestly as I know how, this book does contain a "word from the Lord." The messages in these chapters have been written in love and compassion with no other design than to bless and encourage true Christians. If, in some points, I fail—it is only because my zeal may be greater than my knowledge.

Of one thing I am very certain—my grandfather would call this a "mad-glad" book because it leaves very little middle ground.

Contents

1

Gossip

"Have you heard the latest?"

Gossip is fast becoming the biggest weapon Satan has against God's chosen people. Rumors are flying around everywhere. Filthy gossip is ruining the reputations, ministries, and marriages of many of God's choicest servants.

If I believed all the gossip I overhear daily, I would lose all faith in mankind. Gossip does not always originate in a barroom. It is not all passed on by reprobates and prostitutes. Most of the gossip circulated today pours out of the hearts and lips of Christians who sit in a church pew every Sunday morning singing about the love of Jesus.

Ministers often complain about how certain members of their congregation "talk about them behind their backs." It's a well-known fact that some parishioners go home every Sunday afternoon and "chew up the pastor." They gossip about his new car, his hair, his wife's shoes, his sermon, his "dictatorial methods." And shamefully, many Christian members seem to gloat over a minister who gets caught with another woman or who gets in to some kind of moral, financial, or spiritual trouble.

Satan is out to destroy every man and woman of God, and he will stop at nothing to discredit an effective ministry. Tragically, some ministers are just as guilty of nasty gossip as the members they accuse. They sit around at conventions and in little "after meeting" sessions trading stories of pastors and evangelists who have "messed up." Most of the gossip is vicious, but seldom true.

Recently I was suddenly overwhelmed by all the reports I'd heard of ministers having problems, of marriages breaking up, of evangelists who were reported to be living double lives. It was so depressing; it sounded as if almost everybody was having problems. The world was going berserk.

A well-known young single evangelist had rumors circulated about him suggesting he was a homosexual. Thousands were attending his six-week-long revival meetings, and unusual evidence of God's power was demonstrated. Yet, every time his name was mentioned some minister would pipe up, "Isn't it a shame he's a homo? How can God use him when he's so sweet and effeminate?"

A minister friend of mine resigned his church suddenly. The following week I received three phone calls from "saints" who warned me to have nothing to do with the man "because he had been having an affair with five women in the church." They each insisted he had been forced to resign and that everybody in the country knew why.

A well-respected minister approached me, enlisted my help "to combat the false doctrine being promoted by a certain youth group involved in missions." I was asked to use my influence to expose them and straighten out their thinking. They were reportedly "ruining" young people all over the state of California. I heard the same rumor in every state I visited for the next four weeks. The leader of their missionary youth group was supposed to have indoctrinated other youth leaders and they had "all gone bananas."

While in prayer one night my heart began to cry out, "Oh God! What is happening? Everything seems to be falling apart. False doctrine, immorality, compromise. What shall I do?" And it didn't take God very long to get the answer through to me.

First of all, God began to deal with me about my own gossiping tongue! No one thinks of himself as being guilty of gossip. But I was one of those who always prefaced my gossiping remarks with, "Now I'm only telling you this so you can pray about it. Mind you, I love this person, but did you hear about. . . ?"

We use all kinds of excuses to spread our gossip garbage, and seldom do we stop to think of the far-reaching effect, of the horrible damage, of the ruin we can cause. I suddenly recalled the many times I had passed on rumors. I had joined in the ministerial gossip circles and passed on things I'd heard without a single thread of evidence. Unwittingly, I'd become a tool in Satan's hand to destroy another man's ministry.

God not only forgave me, He put within me a fighting spirit: A desire to stand up and combat a lying devil! A desire to defend God's servants, no matter how vicious the gossip against them. God made me somehow sense what it would be like to be the victim of gossip rather than the purveyor of it. I wanted to go out and shut up the lying, gossiping lips of every parishioner and minister who attempted to ply me full of filth, rumors, stories, innuendoes, or hearsay.

I did a little investigating, too. The evangelist who was rumored to be a latent homosexual confided in a friend of mine, "Being single, I've tried so hard to stay away from all women so as not to bring reproach on my ministry. Now they accuse me of homosexuality. It's simply not true." I believe him! And now, every time I hear anybody spread that rumor I call them on it. I ask them to prove it or shut up!

I called the minister who had resigned his church. I asked him bluntly, "Do you know about the vicious rumor your church is spreading about you? You are supposed to be a ladies' man!"

He answered clearly and quickly, "David, it's simply not true. The people who started that rumor have tried to destroy every pastor before me. God as my judge, it's all a lie." His wife verified the statement. I gave him the names of the people who started the story and offered to help him put them at the mercy of the law. While he prefers to take it quietly, I grieve that a man's ministry is nearly destroyed by satanic gossip.

I met with the leader of that youth organization supposedly preaching "false doctrine." We met in Lausanne, Switzerland. He was gracious and kind as I placed before him all the stories, the rumors, and gossip about his organization. I did so only to ascertain for myself if any of it was true. I found not a single trace of false doctrine. Rather, I found a dedicated young man who was doing more for God than all of the jealous men who had spread the rumors. We prayed together, hugged one another, and I left him with a pledge to stop every word of gossip about him I came across. Since that meeting I've straightened out a number of ministers who had been trapped into believing the gossip.

How many great men and women of God lay prostrate each night, lost in a stream of tears, as they try to understand how and why they are victims of lies and gossip. They give their very lifeblood to the work of Christ, and they have learned to expect satanic attacks when they storm the gates of hell. But there is no hurt like the deep cutting of cruel gossip that is passed on by the very ones who should be encouraging and praying for them. You can fight and resist the devil, but how can you respond and defend against weapons formed against you in the hands of God's own servants who indulge in gossip?

You expect gossip from liars, cheats, and low street people. You expect it in politics and public life. But no gossip is as vicious, as damaging, and as hurtful as that which comes from God's own people out of God's own house. How Satan must laugh with glee when he witnesses "Spirit-filled" people passing on lies and filthy stories that originated in Hell itself.

Satan won't need an army of demons to accomplish his work of deceiving. All he needs is an unwitting army of Christians who give him an ear and a tongue who go about "tattling his tales." Passing on a single bit of gossip can wreck a marriage, shipwreck a ministry, turn loving children against parents, and break the hearts, destroy the dreams, smash the hopes of completely innocent people.

Saints of God, hear me! We can no longer afford the indulgence of gossip. We can no longer allow ourselves to give our lips and voices to the service of Satan to malign, to destroy, to assassinate with gossip. It matters not whether the gossip is true or not. Let God take care of that! It is our part to defend our brothers and sisters in Christ. And even if the most vicious gossip were true, we should be spending all our time and talk in restoring, healing, and lifting up the fallen.

I am absolutely convinced Satan has taken physical control of all rumor mills and gossip mongering. He is out to destroy and discredit all that is of the Holy Ghost. He is out to destroy—with gossip— every Christian who seeks the fullness of God.

Let us not allow it. May God raise up an army of saints whose hearts and lips are baptized and dripping with the honey of God's true love, in honor preferring one another. In Christian charity let us grieve over those who have failed; let us never gloat! We can send the devil into the pits to lick his wounds if we will join together to "stop the gossip." If you can't prove it—don't tell it! If you can prove it—keep it to yourself and pray about it. It will, it must, it can stop with you!

2

Speaking With Tongues

Speaking with tongues is polarizing the organized church!

Too many people today preach that everybody must speak with tongues—and too many others preach that no one should speak with tongues.

My father was a Pentecostal minister, a dedicated man. Our church was not "down by the railroad tracks." It was underneath the tracks. An elevated train ran directly over our little church house. People in that church got happy; they sang and shouted; and they talked in tongues.

We were called "holy rollers," and people looked down their spiritual "noses" when they referred to the poor tongue talkers. I grew up feeling like a second-class Christian, unwelcome by quiet, dignified kinds of worshippers who attended nice, quiet, dignified kinds of churches.

Tongues were not divisive because only Pentecostals experienced and practiced it. Baptists, Methodists, Presbyterians, Episcopalians, Catholics, and others considered it as belonging unequivocally and only to the Pentecostals.

But now tongues have moved uptown. Orthodox Catholics, staid Presbyterians, dignified Episcopalians, and dispensationalized Baptists are now among those in the middle of the charismatic movement.

The last two chapters of *The Cross and the Switchblade,* telling of the Holy Ghost baptisms among addicts and delinquents, helped create new interest in charismatic renewal. *Time* magazine stated, "Everywhere a charismatic renewal happens, inevitably those involved have read *The Cross and the Switchblade* or *They Speak with Other Tongues* (John Sherrill)."

Catholic priests and nuns approach me everywhere I go now, thanking me for writing the book and for contributing to the spiritual hunger created in their hearts that led to a charismatic experience. The same is true of ministers of nearly all denominations. I rejoice in all these wonderful testimonies.

But something worries me! Holy Ghost baptisms are being reported worldwide. Multitudes are now speaking with tongues and praising God! But with it has come division, strife, misunderstanding, and polarization.

On one side, you have those who preach tongues more than Christ; on the other side, those who preach it is "inspired by the devil."

Some teach you cannot be saved unless you speak with tongues; others believe only "unstable psychotics" get into the charismatic movement.

Believers testify their baptism motivated them to go out and meet human need, but critics say they just sit around in "bless me clubs" and "conjure up" the Holy Ghost.

Those who speak with tongues believe they are praising God and edifying their souls. Critics accuse them of unintelligible jabbering and self-deception.

Critics point to the excesses and certain bizarre, fringe, histrionic displays and cannot see any of the genuine. They point to the lack of love practiced by some who speak with tongues. Tongues people are accused of acting "holier" and more "spiritually learned" than those who are not.

I am really grieved by what I see developing in the organized church. The new Jesus people have no hang-ups on the matter of tongues. They love and worship together, and those who speak with tongues are welcomed as brothers and sisters with those who do not.

But not so in organized denominational circles. We talk a lot about love, but we practice a horrible kind of hate—and bitterness is the end result.

I don't understand why tongues have to be an issue. Why can't Baptists, Methodists, Catholics, and Pentecostals all love and fellowship together in Christ's name?

I speak with tongues in my secret closet of prayer. It is a beautiful devotional experience with me. It is not a group or public experience. No one else is involved but Jesus and me! And when a brother in Christ comes to me and says, "I believe I too have a wonderful Holy Ghost baptism, and I've never spoken in tongues," I say, "Praise God—I believe you." Why should there be any argument? We should rejoice in each other's love for Christ.

I believe the Holy Ghost is big enough to take care of Himself. He needs no defense—no super salesman—no public relations director—and no pressure promoting. And I don't believe in "Holy Ghost" specialists who spend their time promoting the gift instead of the Giver.

I don't believe the Holy Ghost makes a fool of anyone. You don't have to scream at Him or try to wake Him from the dead. A true Holy Ghost baptism is a "baptism of love" that helps you see and love a lost world through the eyes of Jesus.

Why then should anyone be forced to leave his church because he speaks with tongues? Why should he suddenly be thought of as "emotionally unstable" because of a deep spiritual awakening? If, contrary to a person's honest criticism, this experience is genuine and of God, is there not danger of speaking out against the Holy Ghost? Suppose there are excesses! Suppose those who speak with tongues try to "infect" the entire congregation. Can we not trust that through patience, love, understanding, and compassionate Bible preaching that God will bring about a stable situation? Isn't the Holy Spirit capable of keeping a balance in spite of all our fears of fanaticism?

Pity the poor Catholic who speaks with tongues. His own church doesn't know how to react. Old-line Pentecostals insist they "leave the harlot mother church." Both conservative and liberal Protestant churches treat them as if they have "spiritual small-pox." They are a people (now over 100,000) without a church! One Pentecostal woman wrote:

"My baptism is from God, but those Catholics are faking it with all that Mary stuff still hanging on. Let them leave the Catholic church like we did."

For the past five years I have refused to speak for the Full Gospel Businessmen. I disagreed with their view of the baptism of the Holy Ghost. It seemed to me they were always pointing to their banner which read, "Our Banner Is Love," while putting down denominations and solid organizations. Businessmen seemed to be saying, "Last year I only made $20,000, but I received the Holy Ghost and now I make $50,000 a year." To me, it appeared to be a special "in group" who traveled the world over to swap stories about deliverances from denominational ties—about financial successes—and prize "catches" for the baptism God had given them. But I see a prejudice in my own heart just as grievous as that of critics who fight them on doctrinal grounds. In spite of their stumbling—in spite of their excesses—God is using them. I want to rejoice with them.

The challenge facing every Spirit-filled person who speaks with tongues is clear. If this experience is all we claim it to be, we must set the example of love. We must practice humility and have a teachable spirit. We must get out on the streets and put it to the test. We must have no part in division or disputes and we must hold in highest honor every Christian brother and sister who interprets the baptism in different ways.

Those who speak with tongues must put the fruits of the Spirit above the gift. A truly baptized Christian will not drink, smoke, curse, or indulge in anything unholy or unChristlike. He must not consider the gift of tongues as a cure-all, end-it-all, best-of-all experience. It is just a starting place. There is so much more. If a person who speaks with tongues honestly believes God is controlling his speech—when he comes back down to earth and speaks with his own understanding, he had better not gossip, back bite, or verbally assassinate another brother. Tongues should be a "Holy Ghost mouthwash."

If speaking with tongues is a gift for today, it must not be put on display like a toy to be played with. It is not a weapon to hurt or destroy with but a gift to unite and edify, and if that is not the result, someone is misusing the gift. Away with thinking that everybody who speaks with tongues is a saint. Away with trying to force it on others who do not seek it. Those who speak with tongues should spend every syllable and sentence talking to God. It should break a man's heart, melt his stubborn spirit, build up his love, and create in him a contriteness and gentleness that all men can recognize. If tongues are a sign to the unbeliever, that is what they should see!

The challenge to those who do not believe in speaking with tongues is also very clear! To say it is of the devil is to impune the morals, the Christian love, the great ministries of thousands who have given their all to the Lord's work. If you have the baptism of the Holy Spirit without an evidence of speaking with tongues, your evidence must be even greater. It must be one of campassion and love—even for those you feel are in error. You must not discount the genuine because a few overzealous people appear to be excessive or out of order.

Do not judge the Biblical experience by the firsthand experience you have had with only a few charismatic believers. Don't harbor prejudice based on books you have read by "experts" who discount it all. Often experts deplore and criticize those who speak with tongues and then protect themselves from being judged or criticized themselves by hiding behind research charts and special degrees. Shake off all fears related to speaking with tongues. To disfellowship former friends who speak with tongues—to put them out of the church—to call them fanatics—is an admission that the Spirit of God in you cannot be called forth to cope with it. It seems ironic that some ministers are willing to cope with the devil but refuse to cope honestly with a "break out" of tongues in the church. That is a cop-out.

I can tell you this: I intend to love every Catholic—those who speak with tongues and those who don't. If they love my Jesus and believe His gospel, they are my brothers and sisters. Our differences may still be there, but the Holy Spirit can overcome all barriers!

I intend to love everybody I come in contact with, from any denomination, whether he accepts or rejects my baptism. I want to respect men of God in every denomination and humble myself until they can look beyond my faults to see Christ's love.

I am praying for a new day, a day of real love when we can say, "In Christ we are one." A day where the upper room does not overshadow the cross. A day when we can lay aside our doctrinal differences and see the Christ in one another. A day in which we no longer call ourselves by some denominational tag, but we all call ourselves simply—The Jesus People! A day when we put aside all controversy and begin "in honor preferring one another." A day we will no longer get hung up on tongues, or modes of water baptism, or manners of sanctification, or measures of grace. But instead work together to save a lost world while it is still day.

Lord, let there be love!

3

Demons

"We know that whosoever is born of God sinneth not [is not a slave to sin]: but he that is born of God keepeth himself, and that wicked one toucheth him not" (I John 5:18).

The Bible makes it positively clear that he who is born of God cannot be ruled or possessed by Satan. And yet we have a growing number of people today who live in constant fear of lurking demons, ready to inhabit their holy temples.

Simultaneous with a growing Jesus movement is a growing devil movement. There is now an alarming emphasis on demons and Satan in charismatic circles. The neodemonism prevalent today suggests Christians can be inhabited with as many as 300 demons. Every problem, every human failure, every disease, every habit is attributed to direct demon influence.

People who suffer from feelings of inadequacy, who believe they are ineffective, and who fight a losing battle against secret sin are especially attracted to this teaching of demon possession. They blame all their trouble and weakness on a "demon" making them do things against their will, and they seek out an exorcist who can, with a single prayer of dominion, end their battle.

Satan is on the loose. He directs an army of spirits and demons united to harass the kingdom of God. Demon possession is a growing phenomenon. Demon-crazed minds are behind the moral landslide—behind all the dirty books and movies, the nudity, the lawlessness, crime and murder. The sinner who confronts this daily baptism of dirt is exposed to demon possession, and there is growing evidence this is happening everywhere. Men and women of God must rise up and take dominion over Satan and every demon that tries to subvert or trap any Christian. Yet we must never forget Satan's power has been limited by God.

Satan cannot possess any person who has been born of God! Demons cannot enter a blood-washed child of Christ! Those who teach otherwise base their doctrine only on human experience. They cannot prove it from the scripture, at all!

Jesus said, "For the prince of this world cometh and hath nothing in me" (John 13:40).

That must be where every true Christian stands. Satan comes against me but has no influence, no power, no entrance—has nothing in me. Satan may enter a Judas, an Ananias or Sapphira, but he cannot enter a Christian unless he first binds the Christ in him and casts Him out.

"Or else how can one [Satan] enter into a strong man's house [Christian heart], and spoil his goods [possess him], except he first bind the strong man [Christ]? And then he will spoil his house" (Matt. 12:29).

God's Word is clear on this subject.

1. It is blasphemy to believe that Satan can bind and cast out the Christ in the believer. Satan does not have access to the mind of Christ in me.

"Every kingdom divided against itself cannot stand—it is brought to desolation" (Luke 11:17).

2. There is only one way for Satan to gain entrance—and that is for a man to cast off his faith and love and turn aside begging for trouble.

"Having damnation, because they have cast off their first faith. For some are already turned aside after Satan" (I Tim. 5:12, 15).

3. The Christian is warned by God's Word to beware of the devices of Satan. But Jesus always distinguished between devices, torments, and possession by demons. They are not the same.

"And his fame went throughout all Syria: and they brought unto him all sick people that were taken with divers diseases and torments, *and* those which were possessed with devils, *and* those which were lunatick, *and* those that had the palsy; and he healed them . . ." (Matt. 4:24).

4. God promises the Christian full protection from sun stroke, moon stroke, and devil stroke!

"The Lord is thy keeper; the Lord is thy shade upon thy right hand. The sun shall not smite thee by day, nor the moon by night. The Lord shall preserve thee from *all evil*: He shall preserve thy soul . . ." (Ps. 121:5-7).

5. Jesus forbade demons to speak out. He demanded they keep silent. That is still the scriptural pattern.

"And devils also came out of many, crying out, and

saying, Thou art Christ the Son of God. And he rebuking them suffered them *not to speak*: for they knew that he was Christ . . ." (Luke 4:41).

"And there was in their synagogue a man with an unclean spirit; and he cried out, saying, Let us alone; what have we to do with thee, thou Jesus of Nazareth? Art thou come to destroy us? I know thee who thou art, the Holy One of God. And Jesus rebuked him, saying, Hold thy peace and come out of him" (Mark 1:23-25).

6. Satan can return only to the vessel unfurnished by the Holy Spirit.

"When the unclean spirit is gone out of a man, he walketh through dry places, seeking rest; and finding none, he saith, I will return unto my house whence I came out. And when he cometh, he findeth it swept and garnished. Then goeth he, and taketh to him seven other spirits more wicked than himself; and they enter in, and dwell there: and the last state of that man is worse than the first" (Luke 11:24-26).

7. Paul warns against allowing the heart to become bound by any yoke—including the yoke of fear and demons.

"Stand fast therefore in the liberty wherewith Christ hath made us free, and be not entangled again with the yoke of bondage" (Gal. 5:1).

So hear me, all ye saints of the Lord.

—Do not fear the devils or his demons.

—Do not accept teaching that is unscriptural.

—Do not lose your joy and freedom in Jesus.

—Do not fret about your battles, illnesses, or afflictions.

"Many are the afflictions of the righteous—but the Lord delivereth him out of them all."

With Christ say, "Satan, get thee behind me."

4

Will Your Teenager Run Away This Year?

Police officials estimate that probably only one in every five parents issues warrants for their runaway kids. With more than 200,000 warrants being issued, this would suggest there are in excess of one million runaway kids in the United States today.

They are mostly white and middle class, the majority coming from broken homes. It is now estimated that one out of every two and one-half marriages ends in divorce. Many educated and well-to-do parents have simply given up on their unruly kids and have allowed them to run off. These parents have thrown up their hands as if to say, "Who needs this? I've got my own life to live, and I'm not going to let an undisciplined child ruin it."

Many of these kids run away from home, they claim, because they cannot accept as important the things parents are addicted to. The kids claim they are choking on an overabundance of materialism that leads to a life of despair. Now they have discovered they can hitchhike and get away from it all. They can take off to rock festivals, hit the streets, and undertake an entirely new life-style. Many of them claim they are not running away from something; rather, they are running to it.

Most runaways cannot intelligently explain why they took off from their homes. They only know they want to get as far away as they can from adults and their hang-ups. And yet many of these runaways trying to escape the materialism of their parents are escaping in high style in carpeted mini-buses complete with a portable refrigerator, hi-fi, and a portable water bed.

Not all runaways come from broken homes. A recent report reveals that some are very much like their non-runaway counterparts from "best" homes —who complain about "strictness of parents who are unrealistic and uncompromising." The second largest number of complaints came from young people who claim they ran away from home because of a hassle over fashions—long hair, funky styles, and hippie-like apparel. Most of these young runaways showed much intolerance and impatience toward parents and were quick to accuse them of weaknesses. Some kids say they ran off simply because their parents would not let them stay out after ten p.m.—so they simply left, not even willing to stick around and try to explain why.

Those of us who work with runaway kids often hear parents say, "But my teenager is not the kind of person to run away. Why, my daughter hasn't even been downtown alone. Why would she try to run away? We thought she was happy and we tried to let her know she had all the freedom she needed."

One parent explained, "We never spanked her, and we always gave her plenty of money. Her closet is full of clothes and some still have the price tags on them. Her room is loaded with plenty of records, and she has her own car. What else does she want? Why did she have to run away?"

Later the same mother offered, "Perhaps we should have given her that maxi coat she wanted. That's the only thing I can think of that could make her mad enough to run away."

Occasionally a runaway will wake up and get honest about his life and why he really ran off. One teenager confessed, "I ran away just to blow off steam. It helped me to see another side of life, but I can tell you it isn't good at all. I would like to go back to school and go back home. I thought kids ran off in search of something, to find themselves, but most of them I have met are in a big rut. They're no better off than suburban kids. All they discuss is drugs and phony trips, and it's just as boring as talk about school dances and big cars. And what about LSD, speed, and pot? At first it is beautiful. Then you learn that it doesn't enlarge your perspective at all, and you have not discovered who you are or where you're going. It's all a bad trip. It would be better to fight it out at home and learn what life is really all about."

Seventeen-year-old Rita said, "Kids sit around in school talking about how nice and loving it is when you run away and live with street people. They talk about free love, free food, and people helping one another. But just get pregnant and see what happens! They want nothing to do with you. You face the cold winter nights without money, friends, or love. They really don't want to get hassled over problems of other people. They might welcome you back when you get over it, and everything is A-OK. Life on the street is supposed to be based upon honesty without rules or regulations. But that's simply not true. There is nothing free, and love is only cheap talk. If you sleep around with the fellows, they might accept you, but they sure cut you off if you don't give in all the time. When the truth is out, you soon find out that life on the street is a one-way ticket to hell."

Now we have a new phenomenon on the American scene—the stay-at-home-runaway. These are the young people who, for one reason or another, choose to stay at home and make it difficult on their. parents—either because of hatred, bitterness, or to get revenge. In a recent survey involving more than 3,000 teenagers in five major cities, better than 50 percent claimed they hated their parents. Not one of them has left home. And yet many of them said they were not even talking to their parents, even though they still lived under the same roof with them.

Many parents are now in a state of panic, afraid their teenager will run off and join the street culture. In an effort to keep them at home and satisfied, they are making all kinds of compromises. They are making it clearly evident to their kids there is no need to run away. Consequently, many teenagers have taken over at home. As one teenager put it, "My dad and mom are scared to death I'm going to run away. Now they let me be my own boss and

I can come and go as I please. I'm really not too mad at them but I want them to think I am. All you have to do is drop a couple of hints about your friends who have run away and my folks just melt like butter. Man, I can even bring my chick into my own bedroom and make-out without being hassled by my parents. They just don't want me to leave. So I can do anything—just so I stay home."

Why should a kid run away from home today at all? There is no more reason to. After all, the parents are ready to make any kind of concession to avoid the trauma and trouble of reporting a runaway kid to the police department.

Fashions are changing so fast now, parents have resigned. Most young people today are allowed to dress anyway they choose, and in many cases Dad and Mother have adopted some of their fashions for themselves. And a great number of parents know they have abdicated their rights to preach morals to their kids because of their own hypocrisy. How can a tobacco chain-smoking father lecture his boy about pot smoking? How in the world can a mother who sips cocktails all day talk to her own teenage daughter about her moral standards? Divorcing, smoking, cheating, drinking parents have been caught in their own immoral trap!

I am convinced that kids do not hate their parents nearly as much as they hate their hypocrisy. One teenage girl said, "I got bitter against my mother because she didn't stand for anything. She couldn't be strict with me because she wasn't strict with herself. She is basically a very weak person and you can't respect weak parents."

The Bible warns against parents "provoking their children to anger." But we are spawning a generation of young people who are learning to despise and hate their parents because of provocations based on fear, guilt, and hypocrisy. Young people are not provoked to anger as a result of firm discipline, honest restrictions, and assigned responsibility. They are provoked to anger by pleasure-loving, self-centered parents who have become so wrapped up in their own pursuits of happiness and who have become so involved in solving their own problems—they have had no time to really understand the heavy problems their own children are stymied with.

Without a doubt the number one youth problem of the future will be HATRED AGAINST PARENTS. I believe it is on the verge of becoming an epidemic, and I predict that it soon will.

For the Christian parents, the problem is often quite different. Children who rebel against Jesus Christ often rebel against their Christian parents. Often teenagers, convicted by their own rebellion against Christ, seek to get away from their praising, "hallelujah" parents. Children who get out of touch with God all too often get out of touch with their parents.

It's true that God-fearing parents often put too much pressure on their children. They overlecture them about church attendance, dress codes, and moral standards. And even though this overzealous concern is based on a love for their eternal souls, this ultraconservative, rigid kind of strictness can lead to a terrible kind of rebellion. Preachers' kids are often among the worst rebels of all.

There is also a danger of religious parents being so involved in the work of God that they neglect their children. I know that for a fact! I have too often taken in as patients the drug-addicted sons and daughters of missionaries and ministers who were so busy doing God's work they had no time for their precious children. Those very same kids went out to the street to find attention, love, and friendship. Later, when those parents try to "make it all up" —it's too late.

The Bible predicts that in the last days, "a man's enemies will be they of his own household." Many God-fearing parents have known the bitter pain and agony of rebelling children who have been caught up in a satanic snare, and the pain is all the worse when those parents know they have done the best they can, have prayed and wept over their children, and committed them to the Lord. Yet, when children become young adults, they must answer to God for themselves. Parents can lead them only so long.

I believe God is going to intervene, otherwise this earth is smitten and doomed. When God's people have done all they know how to do, they are commanded to simply stand still and see the salvation of the Lord. I am firmly committed to the prophecy of Malachi 4:6, and it is there I place all my hopes.

"And he shall turn the heart of the fathers to the children, and the heart of the children to their fathers, lest I come and smite the earth with a curse."

Turn your children over to God—even the runaway! Hold onto the promise: "Train up a child in the way he should go: and when he is *old,* he will not depart from it."

5

The Forgotten Teenager

Drug abuse is now our number one national problem, according to President Nixon. It's talked about on radio, TV, in churches, schools and in nearly every home. Kids who use drugs are analyzed, studied, hospitalized—and they are on the front pages of our newspapers. There is so much emphasis on drug abuse today, people seem to think every high school kid is a pot-head and every college student an acid-freak. Statisticians like to remind us that more than fifteen million Americans experiment with pot and that acid trips on campuses are now a part of college life-style.

But all this spotlighting of drugs—all this preoccupation with problems and addictions is causing a terrible side effect. We are developing in our country a whole new breed of young person. I call him THE FORGOTTEN TEENAGER.

The forgotten teenager is not a junkie. He doesn't smoke pot or drop acid or pills. He is not a radical who runs down his country or who spits on the nation's flag. The forgotten teenager is not hiding out in Sweden to avoid the draft. He is not a hippie on the run; he refuses to split from home. Nor is he hiding in some isolated commune to escape the responsibilities and problems of modern life.

The forgotten teenager is not among the Jesus freaks or even among the honest Jesus rebels. He stands by in silence while they get a billion dollars worth of publicity while cheering for Jesus.

The forgotten teenager is not an alcoholic, nor is he rotting in some prison or rehabilitation center. He is not a criminal or sex fiend. He is not down on his parents, his government, or the church. He is not dressed in funky fashions just to prove something. In fact, he is called square, uncool, straight, or "goodnik." He is made to feel left out, unlearned, unimportant, and very old-fashioned.

You don't have to look very far to find him. He sits in the pew in front of you at church. He sits quietly in the classroom, wondering what's wrong with him. You see, the forgotten teenager is the normal boy or girl who has no hang-ups! He is so normal he is considered a kook. Everybody seems to have forgotten him just because he is good, unfettered by some big habit, and quietly at work being a good citizen, a good child, a good student. And because he doesn't make good copy for the newspaper, he is forgotten in his integrity.

I think we have spent enough time talking about cop-outs, drop-outs, freaks, and runaways. Jesus died for them and I've spent my last fourteen years trying to help all of them I can. But it's high time to recognize the needs and hurts of the normal, forgotten teenager. The needs and problems of normal kids have been overshadowed by rebellion, revolution and revelry. That must be changed—now!

We dare not forget the lost, hopeless child of the ghetto. We cannot forsake the young people who wander aimlessly through our streets, bound by Satan. There is a desperate need for more money, more workers, more compassion and concern to save a whole underground culture of mind-bent youth blinded by heavy habits. But at the same time, we must not neglect that great silent majority of teenagers who are not hooked and shattered, but who now feel no one is concerned about their kind of problems.

A teenage girl came to me recently at the close of a crusade, weeping. She said, "Mr. Wilkerson, you missed me completely in this crusade. For the past three nights you have been preaching about drugs, sex, alcohol, and all your messages were directed to mixed-up, hippie type kids. But what about me? What about thousands more like me? I don't do any of these things. But maybe I should. Maybe I ought to just go out and get stoned, like the others. Because as it is, no one pays attention. Our school counselors only spend time with problem kids. Parents don't have time to talk, unless they suspect you are on drugs and they get worried a little. Who in the world is going to share with me about my problems? You may not think my problems are important—with all your emphasis on those big kind—but to me they are real problems. I'm lonely. My parents and I don't get along. I have terrible doubts about God and I can't seem to figure out where I'm going. I'm just a forgotten teenager."

Let's do something about it, now! First of all,

let us show gratitude in every way possible for kids who have the courage to stand up against the crowd and say, "You can have your drugs and hang-ups. I don't need them. I've found what I've been looking for." A million hallelujahs for every one of them.

Let us quit focusing all our attention on problems. No more panic when drug rumors start spreading. Talk more about the great things our kids are doing; about the Jesus movement; about the thousands of teenagers who now volunteer to do street work helping kids in the ghetto; about cleaning up our rivers and streams, because young people are totally involved; about teenagers who now join missionary tours—who, without pay, are assisting missionaries around the world; about the many teenagers who have organized programs to stop drug pushing in our schools; and about the love and compassion they demonstrate in helping get their friends off hard narcotics.

Let parents, pastors and politicians show a little more trust and confidence in these kids and challenge them to launch their own crusade against drugs and rebellion. At the same time, let the church instill a new kind of Holy Ghost militancy in the hearts of straight Christian kids to combat the satanic militancy we have been exposed to lately.

This is not a whitewash of our growing drug problem. I am not asking that we let down our guard. All I ask is that we all take another look around us and see the multitudes of forgotten teenagers who now reach out to say, "Please don't forget me. I'm here, too."

6

The Forgotten Housewife

A woman writes:

"Dear Mr. Wilkerson, You focused attention on the Forgotten Teenager who feels neglected by all the emphasis on troubled kids—but what about the 'Forgotten Housewife' who feels so unimportant and lost because she has nothing to challenge her?"

This woman dearly loves her husband and three children, and she has never complained about housework or cooking. But she is afflicted with a strange kind of restlessness, especially when she sees so many other women who are doing important things that help change the world.

While the housewife is confined to the house, acting as maid, chauffeur, cook and housekeeper, her husband is out in an active world meeting people and taking part in the important challenge of his work. The housewife is often forced to live in an imaginary world, inventing jobs that no one cares about. The work she does is unnoticed, it changes very little. The food she cooks disappears. What she cleans one day has to be cleaned the next. Her whole world revolves around her husband and her children. And God help her if he stops loving her.

The modern housewife is trapped in a machine world and strangled by schedules. To escape she often seeks relief by spending hours watching daytime soap operas, gossiping with neighborhood wives, or writing trite letters to acquaintances. She then tends to feel guilty and begins to condemn herself. She is relieved from guilt only by launching into a big housekeeping job.

The forgotten housewife is often forced to put up with a "warlord" who believes the only function a wife has is to build him up, heal his wounds, and serve his every whim. This man is convinced he can do anything, his wife can do nothing. He builds his male ego by dwarfing hers. He can't understand that 'trapped' feeling and is convinced he has done enough by giving her "all a woman could want."

He buys her things—gadgets, gifts, and clothes. He wants gratitude. All she wants is a little kindness, slight considerations, and to be noticed once in a while.

She has the kids underfoot all day and night and tries her best to discipline them without losing their love and respect. He comes home, the hero, to claim the hugs and kisses. All too often her best efforts to discipline the children are questioned and she is "put down" for a lack of patience or understanding.

His paunchy stomach and sagging double chin is called muscle. An honest man may even admit he is "pleasantly well rounded." But every pound she puts on is called by its right name—ugly fat! She can spend all day primping to look her best for a night out with her man only to find herself sitting in a restaurant watching him "gawk" at every good looking woman who walks by.

Most forgotten housewives are only slightly amused by the "woman's lib" people. They are not ready to accuse their husbands of being male chauvinistic, sexist pigs. They are not ready to deny all their God-given instincts of motherhood, housekeeper, and wifehood. But they do not want to waste their lives. They do not want to be taken for granted. They do not want to wake up one day, old and tired, only to find emptiness and rejection. They do not want to be "put on the shelf" like a toy to be played with occasionally.

The forgotten housewife has every right to reach out for fulfillment and purpose. She has a right to find a new challenge, to grow, to give, to change. God understands that inner urge. He put it there!

The forgotten housewife, if she is a dedicated Christian, must learn how to sort out her day to allow time for devotions. Any housewife can more than "keep up" with her husband through reading good resource books. Bible reading women soon become good conversationalists because the power transforms them into new women.

My mother, soon after her marriage, determined she would never fall behind my father mentally, spiritually, or in any other way. She spent much time reading books and would underline and memorize important truths. I remember the great respect my preacher dad gained for Mother because of her tremendous intellectual growth. Our congregation never did know it, but most of Dad's sermons were spawned by seed-thought passed on to Dad from Mother's prolific reading. My father's been dead for twelve years, and I am now the recipient of all that tremendous research and resource material.

Praying housewives tap God's reservoir of wisdom and guidance, and it soon shows in all they do. How tragic that so many housewives walk around from room to room trying to think up things to do when God is calling for a little time to be spent in reading and praying.

Along with Bible reading and praying, the real cure for the "trapped" feeling of so many forgotten housewives is the desire to share with others, not just the husband and children. She should consider her home a chapel, and everyone who walks through her doors should find her ready and willing to counsel or pray over spiritual and physical needs. A wife has more to give to her husband and family when she learns how to share herself, meeting the human need of others.

Every decent man can help without affecting his pride or his meal schedule. He can quit dreaming of big surprises and get down to the real job of remembering the little things. He can quit spreading it on; she wants truth and sincerity. He can bring her into his world. Let her meet those important to him. He can stop correcting her in public and give her credit for knowing just a little bit. He can encourage her to seek outlets. God can direct any seeking housewife into worthwhile ministries that really count. And when she does get involved, he can stop making her feel cheap or accuse her of neglect when she gets home too late to put the meal out on schedule.

There are many forgotten housewives who may never be able to change things. They are locked into a situation that will keep them tied down for years. Some must go on living with a husband who doesn't even try to understand, children who do not appreciate her, relatives who reject her, and friends who can't be depended on.

But God has not forgotten her. He waits in that prayer closet to share every hurt and lift every burden. He cares and understands and He promises rest and assurance. He heals attitudes so that anything can be endured. And though weeping may last through the night, joy cometh in the morning!

Ten Ways to Keep the Magic in Marriage

1. Never allow a third party to interfere. This includes friends, family, relatives or strangers.

2. Never correct each other in public. Every public put-down is a wound that heals slowly.

3. Liberate each other willingly. Quit smothering with jealousy, suspicion or fear.

4. Don't worry about understanding one another. Having to be always understood is just a cop-out. No one can ever be completely understood.

5. Refuse to get unequally yoked together with unbelievers. Every soul friend, private or mutual, must share your faith.

6. Remember the little things. The biggest gifts of material things cannot buy love. Tenderness can.

7. Have eyes only for each other. Work at showing one another special attention in public places.

8. Learn how to say, "I'm sorry," and mean it. Don't put it on. Insincerity proves only that you are unforgiving.

9. Accept problems as a normal part of love. Idealism is for poets. Problems will always exist and must be expected.

10. Turn each other over to God for safe keeping. What is kept safe for God is kept safe for you.

7

Liberate Parents

I would like to see dads and mothers form a "Parents Lib" movement. It's time to set parents free. Free from all the expert mumbo-jumbo on how to raise kids. Free from all the guilt complexes that turn mothers and dads into nervous wrecks because they feel they have failed their kids. Free from all the accusations that they are inept, unconcerned, and unloving.

I have four children, three of them teenagers—and I love them dearly. As mother and father, my wife and I pray over them, encourage them, and do everything within our power to make them into responsible, God-loving young adults. We do the very best we can and sometimes worry too much whether or not we are doing the right thing. Sure, we make mistakes! We get angry and even blow up at times. We yell when we should be quietly encouraging. We sometimes wound them by saying the wrong thing at the wrong time.

We try not to spoil them—yet we often see our protective love rob them of initiative and responsibility. It's like that everywhere today as more and more children soak up the luxuries and attention without preparing themselves for the crises of life.

Parents have become the biggest scapegoats of this generation. They are blamed for delinquency, vandalism, homosexuality, drug addiction, and every other problem their children are involved in. Just ask the experts: "Mother did it!" Ask the minister: "It's their parents' fault. Mom and dad failed them."

In many cases that is too often true. Alcoholic, self-indulgent parents have mortally wounded the personalities of their children and have driven them into lives of crime and dissipation. Children have been abused, abandoned, and mistreated by parents from the beginning of time. Not all poor child rearing, however, was done by wicked parents. Solomon, who wrote the handbook on how to raise kids, failed in raising some of his. The two great patriarchs, David and Solomon, fathered and raised some of the wildest boys in recorded history. Some of them killers, in fact.

But I say it is time to quit blaming all the parents for all the failures of children. I believe most parents do love their children and are doing their dead-level best to raise them with respect and dignity. We do our children a terrible disservice by letting them go scot-free and placing all responsibility on the shoulders of the parents.

Now that I have had fifteen years of hearing the confessions of kids gone wrong, I have come to the conclusion the majority of them have never taken time to see anything good in their parents. They know all the alibies and excuses, the very ones society has provided them. If I am to believe all I hear, none of their parents understood them, none had any good qualities, and they were all complete failures. I can't accept that!

Raising children is getting more and more complicated and difficult. I heard one old-timer say, "Just love kids and pray for them and everything will turn out right." That is not always true. Lot's wife was lost even though that great man Abraham prayed for her. It is possible for parents to do everything right and still lose their children in the later teen years because of the negative influence of evil companions.

I believe in the Bible way of raising children. We are not to provoke our children to anger—not even over fashions, long hair, and personal habits. Our firm discipline must be balanced with love. We must not leave our children to their own devices lest they bring us to shame. We must raise them in the fear and respect of God by setting a good example.

God expects Christian parents to pray diligently over each child so they will "be kept from the wicked one." We must point them to the Word of God for instruction and direction. Then having done all the Lord has commanded—having loved and disciplined the best they know how, having gone the second mile with the children—*parents must then be liberated.*

Away with looking back at mistakes. Parents are human, too. There is not a perfect parent on the earth. God overrules every mistake of sincere parents who know how to pray. The time comes in each home when parents must turn their children over to God and say, "Lord, I'm trying to do my very best. Now you take over. Deal personally with my children as you did with me."

Sometimes children rebel. They turn against parents and they live in bitterness for years. But God's Word is still true. "Train up a child in the way he should go: and when he is old, he will not depart from it" (Prov. 22:6).

That is the promise: "When he is old . . . he will come back."

I am a liberated parent. All my guilt and all my failures have been left at Calvary. I give myself wholly to the Lord and to the love of a good wife. She has been a good mother and she's to be liberated, too. So should all mothers and fathers who love God and are called according to His purpose.

8

To The President

Dear Mr. President:

The American people have given you their vote of confidence. Christians throughout the land pray God will divinely guide and strengthen you in the critical months ahead. We pray for peace in the war against drug abuse.

Drug addiction has enslaved thousands of our young people here at home as well as soldiers overseas, in Europe and Asia. I agree with you that drug abuse is now our number one youth problem. We believe you are truly sincere when you tell those of us working in the drug abuse field that something has to be done now to stop its cancerous growth.

Teen Challenge is just one of many programs geared to help. It is a very confusing problem, and every drug expert has his own pet theory on what must be done. You have probably been blessed and cursed by the many well-meaning specialists who suggest their program is the answer and deserves government money to fund it. After fifteen years

I have given up trying to make any sense out of all the confusion about how we got into this problem and how we should get out.

I am not one of those experts. And we do not want any government money for our program. We American people must quit looking to the federal government as some kind of a god or miracle working machine that can solve problems simply by coughing up enormous amounts of money. Money cannot buy a cure. Fort Knox does not store enough gold to effect the cure of a single addict.

I should also realize that you, Mr. President, are a human being and cannot overnight erase a problem brought on by all of us over a period of years. Our own permissiveness and adult hypocrisy is to blame. You as President cannot be expected to come up with a magic formula or a spectacular cure program when in truth the battle must be waged by every adult and student in the land. No program he offers will work unless we all share the blame and together work on a cure.

I believe God is concerned about this tragic problem, and He alone can solve it. Great religious leaders of history always look to God for solutions in time of national crises.

Government advisors call for a nation-wide methadone program. The narcotics people in Washington have now directed government funded programs to adopt methadone treatment. I'm glad we are not under their jurisdiction because methadone is terribly wrong. It destroys the motive to be cured. It is a substitute narcotic that maintains addicts as cripples for the rest of their lives. It is an admission of defeat and methadone addicts are dying of over-doses. The program is being abused by physicians who start kids on the program, kids who lie about their drug use and should never be given methadone. These same kids end up with a drug problem worse than ever. Thousands of youth now experimenting with narcotics will go on to become mainline addicts using hard drugs because they know methadone treatment will be waiting. Also, methadone users all too frequently still use hard drugs in addition to their methadone treatments. Almost all the arguments favoring the use of methadone have to do with economics alone. The program is morally wrong because it does not insist on or end up in a cure.

There is a way out. It is the most proven, documented cure in existence in our land today. It is the Jesus way, effected by faith in God. Thousands of former addicts testify to the effectiveness of a spiritual cure. Spiritual programs have produced cures at a rate of more than 100 to 1 over all other existing programs.

This is not an oversimplification. Drug abuse is a spiritual, moral problem that will respond only to a spiritual, moral approach. I realize as our President you must represent all the people, including those who cannot accept Christ as the cure. But, is there any written or unwritten law in the land that would prohibit our President declaring drug abuse a spiritual problem and issuing a challenge to the entire religious community? More than a challenge, it should be a call for a spiritual awakening. Young people are in a mood to respond to such a presidential call. In fact, the awakening has already begun. Now is the time to tie the drug abuse problem into the spiritual movement. These kids who now carry Bibles to school can do more to drive drug pushers and abusers from our school corridors than all narcotic agents combined. An estimated 300,000 students have already quit using drugs since the Jesus movement hit the campuses in recent months.

I am encouraged. We are not going to lose this generation to drugs. However, what we need now, Mr. President, is your public encouragement for the spiritual movement among youth throughout the land. Tell those 'God kids' to go to it. Drug abuse is a youth problem, and they have the power to overcome it.

Now is the time to heed the words of the Lord, "If my people, which are called by my name, shall humble themselves, and pray, and seek my face, and turn from their wicked ways; then will I hear from heaven, and will forgive their sin, and will heal their land" (II Chron. 7:14).

David Wilkerson, Executive Director

Teen Challenge, Inc.

9

Money Raising

A lady writes:

"Mr. Wilkerson, please remove my name from your mailing list. Your monthly appeal sounds like a Madison Avenue touch. If yours is a ministry of faith, why not just trust God? Why tell me about your need? You'll never get another dollar from me!"

Now that hurts, and I'll tell you why. I've never before publicly said what I now intend to say. But I think it's time. Each year, New York Teen Challenge and David Wilkerson Youth Crusades must pray in nearly two million dollars just to provide for the ministries God has entrusted to us. In fourteen years God has never once failed us. The sources of our income are absolutely miraculous, especially since no rich people are involved. It comes from people who read *The Cross and the Switchblade* and are moved upon to send a gift.

Visitors who come to see our work firsthand become permanent supporters. A few churches send us regular monthly missionary offerings. But the bulk of our support comes from people all over the United States and Canada who are on our mailing list. Names are collected in crusades, film rallies and by sending in for information.

We send out a newsletter and a magazine, alternating each month. A personal letter goes out with each issue outlining our goals and expressing our most urgent needs. We try not to come on strong, and much time and prayer is spent choosing the most inoffensive appeal at the end of each letter.

There are times when I am writing these appeal letters I ask myself, "How can I ask these people to give again? I have to keep coming back to them every month. How can I tell them about my burden without appearing to be a beggar?"

But let me tell you how I really feel—in the depth of my soul! True Spirit-filled Christians should never be offended by any appeal from God-ordained ministries. It should be considered an honor, a holy trust, to be one chosen by the Holy Ghost to uphold those in the frontline of evangelism with prayers and gifts.

Living by faith is actually living off God's faithful. Vibrant ministries would die without the regular transfusion of missionary offerings. If God seeks for cheerful givers, how can any loving Christian throw that appeal in a wastepaper basket and exclaim, "Just another money letter from those people again"?

I learned a lesson on giving I'll never forget. My wife and I were invited to the Walter Hovings for dinner. He is president of famous Tiffany's in New York and a good friend of ours. On the way to their exclusive residence, I looked up at all the subway signs appealing for help. The Red Cross wanted donations, as did the Cancer Fund, the Multiple Sclerosis Fund, the Boys Clubs, the Heart Fund. During the course of our dinner I told Mrs. Hoving about all those appeal signs, and my next comment was to be, "Isn't it awful—all those hands outstretched for dollars. You can't even ride the subways without getting hit up." But thankfully, before I could say it our beautiful hostess said, "Isn't it wonderful! Isn't it great to live in a country where people can share their needs so freely? Isn't it wonderful to live where we can make enough to help them all a little bit? Isn't it great?"

I felt so ashamed! And some Christians, reading this, should feel ashamed, too, for the same kind of attitude toward all the appeals that come through their mailboxes.

Before you throw that appeal letter and enclosed envelope in the basket and walk away, think about this:

There is a man, called and ordained by God, who looks to you for help to keep his heart from breaking. God put a burden on his heart. He shared that burden with others who forsook all to go with him into his field. Those workers have families, children who need school clothes and Christmas toys, like all other children. They get less in a whole month than most workers get in a single week.

That man of God and all his helpers go out into the highways and hedges to obey a divine obsession. They see firsthand the devastation and terror of satanic powers. The faces of lost souls haunt them into waking hours. They see hungry people and they want to feed them. They see orphans and they want to take them in. They see the naked and want to clothe them. They walk the ghetto streets risking their lives, and what they see and hear marks them for life. The mother of a month-old baby who is afraid to sleep at night because rats get into the baby's crib and bite the child. Sad-eyed little children who wait all day and all night for a prostitute mother or drug-addicted father to come home to feed them. And when they don't come the welfare workers do and off they go to the children's shelter.

Do you know what it's like to hold in your hand a stack of due bills for food, clothing, and the bare essentials of a caring minstry—with not one cent left to pay them—and more food bills to face next week?

Do you know what it's like to get up early, rush to the post office and anxiously reach for the mail, excitedly slit each envelope open and pray over each one, "Dear Lord, meet our need today"? I've done it many times.

Like us, almost every God-ordained ministry has enough people who receive their appeal mail to more than meet every need if all would help just a little. It is not a few giving much, but many giving a little. So many times I get on my knees and cry to God, "Lord, you know our needs. There are more than enough people who knew about it to help! Do a miracle and lift this load."

Tragically, only the same few respond and hundreds simply ignore or act too busy to care.

I think I am going to quit apologizing for needing

help! I'm not going to worry anymore about those few who keep getting offended by reading of our constant and continuing need.

We are not spending any of God's money foolishly. We account for every single dollar. We do not get bogged down with expensive and unnecessary programs or building projects. We are helping people!

You should never support us, or anyone else, unless you can give joyfully. You must feel confident we are honest and will faithfully use your gift to do God's work—His way. You owe it to us, and to yourself, to request we drop you from our mailing list if you cannot at least feel we are worthy of your prayer support. If you cannot send us a dime, you can pray for us and we would so much like you to continue on our list. And if you are not interested in our work with addicts and troubled kids, you will save us needed money by letting us know, especially if we offend you in any way.

To the hundreds of faithful friends and supporters I can bow my head in gratitude and bless the Lord for you! You have added years to our life. You have made the promises of God stand true. You have, through us, fed the hungry, visited the prisoner, clothed the naked. And for all of that God promises to remember it on the judgment day.

10

The New Church

You have heard rumors that the church is dead. That faith is almost gone! That liberals and agnostics have robbed our young people of confidence in a virgin-born Christ! Don't believe it! It is not true!

It's been said that thinking young people have turned to science, that recent moon missions have forced our young people to discount all miracles! Some believe God doesn't stand a chance with teenagers in an age of scientific discovery. Smug atheistic teachers and professors now write books stating emphatically that the church has lost its hold on the young, that Jesus has become just another man, that intelligent kids no longer accept the idea of a supernatural God!

Don't believe it! They are in for a surprise.

It is claimed that millions of young people have left, or are leaving, the church. That the church is full of hypocrisy—rich, and fat, and lazy. That it's more interested in big fancy buildings and real estate investments. That ministers no longer preach the true Gospel but substitute good thinking and social involvement. That kids are fed up with the deadness, the coldness, the childishness, the narrow-mindedness of the church!

It all depends on what church you are talking about! The old church *is* dead. The formal, cold, lifeless, gutless, clubhouse church has no chance at all to reach this generation! As far as kids are concerned, that big, old, rich, cold church IS dead!!

But there is a new church being born! It's THE FIRST CHURCH OF JESUS CHRIST FOR ALL PEOPLE.

This new church doesn't revolve around buildings. It's made up of Jesus people who have cleaned up and invited the Lord to make their bodies His temple!

The members of this new church worship anywhere: in homes, on the beach, in school, out in the country, anywhere two or three of them get together.

They prefer $50 guitars to $50,000 organs. They prefer sitting on the floor or folding chairs rather than on expensive padded pews. They prefer going to meetings in clean, informal clothes rather than the latest fashion. Why? Because they meet to see Jesus rather than to see friends or just to be seen in church to maintain social class.

This new church doesn't care what kind of old church you belong to! The new Holy Ghost church is so full of love that every kind of Protestant can worship Jesus with every kind of Catholic!

The old church was fragmented, going around saying, "Join my church or you won't get to heaven." It turned off kids by pushing all kinds of pet doctrines, church rituals, and man-made rules!

The new church says to all: We can be one in Jesus. Let's reconcile our differences. Let's not fight anymore. Let's all come to Jesus and love and worship Him! Let's go hand in hand into the world and witness about Christ! Let's not push membership in the old church as much as membership into the body of Christ!

This new church doesn't go around boasting about how many members it has! This new church has been delivered from the pressure of numbers and figures and big crowds.

The new church is made up of Calvinists and Arminians who deeply love one another, of Methodists, Episcopalians, Catholics, Baptists, Pentecostals—all bound together in the Holy Spirit, looking for the coming of Christ.

This new church wants to be remembered for its fruits more than its gifts. It is no ordinary church displaying an ordinary love. It is a supernatural, Spirit-directed church exercising a celestial love given by the Holy Spirit.

The new church no longer asks, "Which church is right?" because now the only honest answer is, "Only Jesus is right."

Don't worry about its future either. Don't fret about its holiness, its social concern, or its many other weaknesses. The Holy Spirit who called out this movement "upon sons and daughters" will keep and purify it with the fires of persecution already beginning to set in!

No more God games. No more judging godly success by row upon row of shining Sunday school buses or bulging numbers on the roll. Committees are definitely out and dignitaries have no prestige or favor.

No name evangelist or pastor is in charge and no pope, bishop, or church council has an iota of influence over it!

It is not a hippie church. It is not a freak-out pad either. The Holy Ghost is taking charge now, and changes are happening fast and furiously. Kids are hugging parents and saying, "I love you." Styles are getting closer to center, and sex and drug abusers are commanded to fall in line with the Word of God. Even cigarette smokers are getting convicted. It's a Holy Ghost mouthwash and a thorough house cleaning of body and soul.

Soon the froth will vanish, the fadists will fade away, the "joy poppers" will seek other "truth," the insincere will give up. But then will be left a hard core of young believers no longer afraid of the church or the establishment and back they will come as God's Holy Ghost army to challenge hypocrisy and phoniness. It will force the established church to get its message off the drawing board. It will bring back tears and worship, praise and love, truth and righteousness. It will bring Jesus back to the church and drive out all the rock concerts, the God games, the leftist programing, and it will isolate and render powerless every minister who denies Christ's virgin beginning. Meanwhile, Jesus will come!

11

The Last Christians

I am absolutely convinced we are the last Christians of the world! Jesus is coming. Armageddon is coming. Judgment is coming. And we are the last Christians, living in the last days, witnessing the last events.

The last Christians are going to face tests and trials no other generation has faced. And I'll tell you why! Satan knows the church of Jesus Christ has had years now to build defenses against his age-old methods of deception! We have learned how to overcome worry, how to obtain peace of mind, how to claim power over sickness and disease! We have become pretty efficient on how to know the will of God, how to think positively, how to use the gifts of the Spirit! We have studied the devil. We have written and read thousands of books on how to do almost everything!

But while we have been learning how to cope with his old devices, Satan has subtly tried to lead the last Christians into a strange world alive with new and exotic kinds of tests, trials, and temptations!

Remember, God's Word warns that Satan will

come at the very end "as an angel of light to deceive, if it were possible, even the elect—the chosen of God. . . ."

Now, how could Satan ever deceive, or attempt to deceive, the chosen last Christians? Will he somehow get them into drugs? Acid? Pot? Pornography? Nudity? Alcohol?

Never! That satanic attack is failing!

Will thousands of young last Christians turn to devil worship? To Ouiji boards? Tarot cards? Seances? Fortune telling?

Never! The devil will always be repulsive to normal, believing Christians. Satan can never attract the masses.

Will thousands of young last Christians suddenly go sex crazy? Will they flock to dirty movies? Devour pornographic books? Become homosexuals? Lesbians? Sadists? Illegitimate babies? Free sex and love?

No! As long as the Spirit of God still strives with men, last Christians will keep their morals! This generation has not lost its head about sex and morals.

Will young last Christians leave the church? Will they lose their faith? Become agnostics? Atheists? Abandon all the faith of their fathers? Become intellectual God haters?

Never! Just the opposite is happening! A Jesus movement is capturing unbelievers. College and high school students now want to believe. God is back in school—very obvious and at work.

Not drugs. Not sex. Not rebellion. Not agnosticism. Not satanism. But three beautiful, legitimate, wonderful, innocent things; things we would least expect to get to us!

The last Christian is going to be tested by a devil who comes as an angel of light, so subtle, so innocent, so indefinable, so camouflaged few will recognize what is happening to them! As I see it, these three legitimate things Satan will use to try and deceive the last Christian are prosperity, pleasure, and parents.

None of these three things are sinful or harmful in themselves. But the Bible makes it very clear the devil will use all three as his final weapon to deceive the elect last Christians!

Let me show you how it's already working.

Consider prosperity first. Satan knows exactly what the Bible says about this church age as shown in Revelation 3:14-17.

"And unto the angel of the church of the Laodiceans write; These things saith the Amen, the faithful and true witness, the beginning of the creation of God;

"I know thy works, that thou art neither cold nor hot: I would thou wert cold or hot.

"So then because thou art lukewarm, and neither cold nor hot, I will spue thee out of my mouth.

"Because thou sayest, I am rich, and increased with goods, and have need of nothing; and knowest not that thou art wretched, and miserable, and poor, and blind, and naked."

God's Word warns there will be last Christians who are halfhearted, rich, prosperous, and in need of nothing, not knowing they are wretched, blind, and naked!

There is nothing evil or sinful in being prosperous

and successful. Most of the partiarchs were wealthy men. Abraham was the father of us all and of him the Bible says, "And Abram was very rich in cattle, in silver, and in gold" (Gen. 13:2).

The Bible calls Job a man who feared God and stayed away from evil, but it also says, "Job was immensely wealthy, for he owned 7,000 sheep, 3,000 camels [equivalent to 3,000 mack trucks today], 500 teams of oxen, 500 female donkeys, and many servants and a great house. He was, in fact, the richest cattleman in that entire area . . ." (Job 1:2, 3, Living Bible).

God actually delights in prospering His children! Psalm 35:27 says, "Let the Lord be magnified, which hath pleasure in the prosperity of his servant. . . ."

In fact, there is a law of God that works without fail. God blesses all who give willingly (Mal. 3:10, 11). If all the blessings being heaped on the last Christians are from God, how can Satan use them to deceive and destroy? If I read my Bible right, God blesses a man or a people to prove them! Just as surely as poverty and affliction can test a man, more so can prosperity and fullness of bread. God proved the children of Israel with prosperity and fullness. "Then said the Lord unto Moses, Behold, I will rain bread from heaven for you; and the people shall go out and gather a certain rate every day, that I may prove them, whether they will walk in my law, or no" (Ex. 16:4).

In the vision of my mind, I see Satan appearing before God one last time as he did to accuse Job! But this time to ask permission to tempt the last Christian! Is this how it would be?

"And the Lord said unto Satan, Where have you come from? Satan answered, From going to and fro in the earth and observing the last Christians!

"And the Lord said unto Satan, Have you considered these last-day Christians, how dedicated, how upright, how God-fearing and Christ-loving they are? How they try to run from evil plots?

"Then Satan answered the Lord, Yes, but just take away the hedge you built around them. Job wouldn't forsake you in his poverty, but just increase and bless them far beyond anything Job ever had and see what happens. Make them all affluent like Job. Build them fancy new homes; give them fine automobiles, all the money and gadgets they need, campers, boats, world travel, fine clothes, exotic foods, land holdings. See what happens to your last Christians when they get rich, full, increased with goods and are in need of nothing. They will forget God."

That is exactly what happened to King Hezekiah. "But Hezekiah rendered not again according to the benefit done unto him; for his heart was lifted up: therefore there was wrath upon him, and upon Judah and Jerusalem" (II Chron. 32:25).

There is a saying, "Piety gave birth to Prosperity, then the daughter divorced her mother. . . ." Holy people usually become prosperous and many forget the Lord who blessed them.

Young person, watch out. Your car, your clothes, your motorcycle can be a bigger hindrance than drugs, sex, or alcohol if you become attached or obsessed with them. You can be so wrapped up in materialism you become a lukewarm Christian— blind, weak, and spiritually naked.

Don't go running off to some commune to live like a poor hermit. You can be just as proud of giving everything up and just as miserable as some who have everything.

I see the devil standing back and laughing at some with glee! "Money-mad Christians. Clothes hogs. Security bug got you? Make lots of money. Buy all new furniture. Get bigger cars. Get two or three of them. Buy, plant, sell, marry, divorce. It ruined Lot's generation. It destroyed Noah's generation. It'll get you, too. You well-paid, easy-living, big-eating Christians will get lazy, lukewarm, and be easy prey for me. God, pour it on them. It's getting to a lot of them. . . ."

Have you been infected by prosperity? Are you more interested in your kingdom than God's kingdom? Now, within the hour, lay everything you have at Jesus' feet. Thank Him for all these things, all you own. Then give them back to Him.

Learn to worship and praise His name in the midst of blessings, not just in crises and trouble, but when all is well. There is nothing you own that God wants. Not your new house, car, clothes, speed boat, or surf board. He owns the cattle on a thousand hills. He only wants all of you—your love, your praise, your trust.

Now consider *pleasure*. The Bible warns that in the last days, "Men would become lovers of pleasure more than lovers of God . . ."

It appears many last Christians who were lovers of God are going to be shipwrecked by love for pleasure. Lovers of God find no pleasure in drugs, illegitimate sex, alcohol, tobacco, or smut. Satan knows that! Most of these fleshly pleasures offend and repulse the Christian! What kind of pleasure, then, will Satan try to deceive the Christian with?

Would you believe, leisure time? This has nothing to do with the weeks you spend on vacation. It's not the time you spend touring Europe or the Holy Land. It's not that hunting or fishing trip. It's not the hours you spend surfing or boating, water skiing or horseback riding. No! I believe these things are all good. All these experiences can be enjoyed by all Christians better than sinners. Sinners don't know how to enjoy these good things from God.

I'm talking about all the wasted time. At-home hours, everyday time. The time you could be in God's Word. Time you should be spending in the secret closet. But here comes Satan again accusing you before God, "Look at the last-day Christian, the TV addict. Look at him, at her, hours and hours for soap operas, comedies, sports. No time to get alone with God. He turns God off with a dial. He hunts, fishes, travels, plays golf, and tennis, and basketball. But no time to read and pray. Is that the last-day Christian who walks by faith and not feelings?"

God has given you enough time to even watch TV. He does not condemn you for using the legitimate things of the world. He made time for us to enjoy all travel, sports, socializing, even exciting vacations.

But God never intended these things to consume us, to drive Him out of our time, our hearts and minds.

I cannot honestly name a single legitimate pleasure God wants to take away from any Christian.

But we are surely gorging ourselves on allowable things that rob us of our hunger for God.

The Rapture is going to catch a lot of last Christians unaware. They have become Holy Ghost swingers. Party loving, socializing gad-abouts who can't find one hour anymore for intercession and weeping in a secret closet.

The number one sin of the last Christian is WASTING TIME. The devil doesn't have to trap you in sex, drugs, drink, or doubt. All he has to do is *keep you busy.* Too busy for God. We are not so much sinners to God as much as we are strangers to God.

The greatest sin against God is not abusing the body, or indulging the flesh, or even cursing His name. The greatest sin against God is simply to ignore Him.

Of the wicked, the Psalmist said, "God is not in their thoughts." It's ironic. Christians who lived so far from the judgment day, so far from the return of Christ, prayed, fasted, and devoured the Word of God. But the last Christian, so close to judgment, so close to Christ's return, so in need of God's help, spends the least time of all in His presence.

Why didn't Noah's message get through to that generation? Because they were so in love with the pleasures of buying, planting, selling, and love making.

Finally, *parents.* Satan is now using unconverted members of your family to drag you down.

The Bible clearly predicts life and death problems in the home just before Christ returns. In Matthew 10:21 it is stated, "And the brother shall betray brother, and the father the child: and the children shall rise up against their parents." And in Matthew 10:36, "And a man's enemies shall be they of his own household."

Listen very closely to the warning of Jesus! "For I am come to set a man at odds against his father, and the daughter against her mother, and the daughter-in-law against her mother-in-law."

Jesus is saying, "If you follow me, your father or mother may never understand. They may resist you and be against you at every turn. Those in your family who do not follow me will be against you once you give me your all. Your worst enemies may be right in your own house. They may even hate you."

There is one Bible story that illustrates this perfectly in John 9:1-23.

Here is the story of a young man who was born blind. Jesus had compassion on him, made a mud pack with His own spittle, and put it on his eyes. He was told to wash it off in the pool of Siloam.

The establishment Jews were incensed because Jesus healed him on the Sabbath. They grabbed the boy's parents and questioned them. Now listen to what his parents answered because it is typical of what is happening in homes everywhere today: "His parents feared the Jews, so they answered, By what means he now seeth, we know not; or who opened his eyes, we know not: he is of age, ask him, he can speak for himself."

These parents did not know Jesus. They knew nothing of His power, or how He could open blind eyes. They were not believers. They were afraid to stand up.

Look at what is happening today. Thousands of young people are once again seeing. Christ is opening the blinded eyes. Those blinded by drugs, sex, etc., are now getting their eyes opened.

But not so with their parents. It's a youth awakening. Parents are afraid. They don't know what to think. Oh yes, they know their kid was blind, and they know a miracle has happened. But their bridge club friends—their business partners—they are too afraid to own up to Christ's power.

The kids know Jesus, but the parents often do not. So it's a house divided.

Satan will try to use your love for parents to rob you of your love for Jesus.

Matthew 10:37 states, "He that loveth father or mother more than me is not worthy of me. . . . He that loveth son or daughter more than me is not worthy of me. . . ."

Jesus was talking about trouble between parents and children when He referred to taking up a cross: "And he that taketh not his cross, and followeth after me, is not worthy of me. . . ." For some of you, the biggest cross you have to bear is your own loved ones. Parents or children. You must love and obey Jesus more than you love and obey your parents.

Jesus Himself said to His mother, "Know you not that I must be about my Father's business?"

Young person, don't let the devil use your family to get you discouraged! Love and obey and respect your parents, but never allow them to take anything from you Jesus has given. Put Him first, above *every* member of your family.

Never, never, never follow the bad example of

parents who do not know Jesus! Parents are *not* always right.

So then, Christ's message to every last Christian is simply this: Don't be condemned by too many things or too much fun or leisure. "There is now therefore no condemnation to them who are in Christ Jesus, who walk not after the flesh, but after the Spirit." But seek first the kingdom of God and His righteousness. Then *all* these other things shall be added without condemnation.

Let no one (even parents) or no thing stand between you and complete surrender and trust in Jesus!

12

Ministration or Ministry

A true Holy Ghost analysis of spiritual ministries is found in the first four verses of Acts 6. In these verses there is a very clear description of the four stages that all Holy Ghost movements go through!

Simply stated, they are: stage one, multiplying; stage two, murmuring; stage three, ministration; stage four, ministry.

And if any spiritual program of God gets shipwrecked or sidetracked, it is because it never gets past stage three. Stage three sets in like rigor mortis and the institution becomes a lifeless social agency.

Let's examine the "Jerusalem Apostolic Home for Widows."

"And in those days, when the number of the disciples was multiplied, there arose a murmuring of the Grecians against the Hebrews, because their widows were neglected in the daily ministration. Then the twelve called the multitude of the disciples unto them, and said, It is not reason that we should leave the word of God and serve tables. Wherefore, brethren, look ye out among you seven men of honest report, full of the Holy Ghost and wisdom, whom we may appoint over this business. But we will give ourselves continually to prayer, and to the ministry of the word" (Acts 6:1-4).

Stage one: Multiplying. This stage is *all growth.*
Every movement has a period in its history that
reads: "And in those days, the number of their disciples was multiplied."

It's the glamour stage—winning favor among all
the people. Problems are dealt with supernaturally.
Ananias and Sapphira fell dead. People are in awe
at the power of God that marks each new effort.

Sacrificial gifts keep the work going ahead. Workers sell all they have and join the dedicated band.
Its reputation spreads all over the world. It is Pentecost in action.

The founders, the original apostles of the movement, have learned to expect miracles. Everybody
is busy waiting on tables of human need. It's an
active stage and there appears to be nowhere to go
but up! The biggest problem is how to find room at
the tables for all the new converts.

Stage two: Murmuring, the problem stage. This
stage is as inevitable as death. In the Herculean task
of feeding the needy, the honeymoon was suddenly
over! The glamour vanished. Problems appeared and
there was an outbreak of discontent. *"There arose
a murmuring at the Grecians against the Hebrews."*
An ethnic, racial problem. An accusation of prejudice. Converts murmuring against staff. Either they
took in more widows than they could handle or else
no more big gifts were coming in. The Bible makes
it clear that *"their widows were neglected."*

Knowing how Paul and Barnabas disagreed and
understanding the temperament of these Pentecostal
staff people, I am convinced there was also much
discontent among them. Things have a way of pyr-
amiding. The source of money is squeezed, important

needs go unmet, converts complain, the staff gets uneasy, and the director gets the blame.

They were no longer in one accord, in one place, with all things in common. The mighty, rushing wind gave way to the whisper of a murmur.

Stage two is pregnant with disaster. The children of Israel took forty years to pass through the murmuring stage. God had to allow all complainers to die off and raise up a new generation with fresh vision. Stage two has been the death of many great works. It has caused churches to sit around powerless for years.

But God allows stage two to purify and test His work to see if its members will buckle down and use these problems as an opportunity to put their trust in Him to perform miracles.

But tragically, we move from stage two to stage three like sheep led to the slaughter. Pay particular attention to this stage because the Holy Spirit has prompted me that we are there now.

Stage three: Ministration, an obsessive preoccupation with waiting on tables! These Spirit-filled, compassionate, heartbroken apostles had to call an emergency membership meeting because they didn't like what was happening to them. *"Then the twelve called the multitudes of the disciples unto them, and said, It is not right for us that we should leave the word of God and serve tables."*

They were not afraid of table work, but they were alarmed because they had become so wrapped up in ministering they were forced to leave off the Word and prayer.

They were becoming called men who could no

longer do more than social work, as important as it was! I can't believe these apostles ever quit praying or studying the Word, but they had been forced to do it in "snitches" and "snatches." Quickie prayers and hurried Bible reading.

Human need had been thrust upon them; growing numbers of converts clamored for their love and attention. Food bills had to be met. Beds had to be furnished, and only eternity will reveal how deeply involved these twelve apostles had become in feeding, housing, and caring for widows.

But no God-ordained work can survive as a Holy Ghost institution when its directors get lost in a maze of file cabinets, bills, plans, and pressing projects. Holy Ghost fired men refuse to allow their spirits to "dry up" in the hustle and bustle of doing God's work even though based on love and compassion.

Those whom God has raised up to head a work must look in His mirror and examine themselves. Priorities have to be straightened out—even if it takes a membership meeting, even if it means appointing special business managers such as these men did at their meeting. "Look out for seven good men of honest report, full of the Holy Ghost and wisdom, whom we may appoint over this business."

Brethren, we must at all cost set our leaders free from business details so they can find time to keep in the flow of the Spirit. And, in turn, every apostolic minister must be willing to let go of those business reins and let a "business apostle" take over. He must not think it will fall apart without him monitoring every transaction. If we will obey the Holy Spirit about stage three, we can joyfully move on to stage four.

Stage four: Ministry. These men of God so loved the kingdom they would not allow it to be shipwrecked by a lack of spiritual power. And they knew where the power came from. They understood why the problems were mounting and why neglect had set in. It was their responsibility to get back to spiritual things.· God had shut the heavens for a short season to get His message through. It is the same message Jesus delivered to busy, hustling Martha. She envied the worshipping Mary who sat at Christ's feet while she waited on tables. But Jesus sided with the quiet, contemplating Mary. "Martha, you are troubled over many things . . . but Mary has chosen the right way . . . these other things ought not to be left undone . . . but first . . ."

Our calling is not first to addicts, widows, the weak and poor. Our ministry is first and foremost to Christ! We are called first to His praise and glory. To meet His need before we feed the multitudes. As we minister to Him, we are at the same time drinking in life, power, resources, direction, ability, and all that is needed to bless the heart of God and in turn meet the world challenge.

God gave me a beautiful insight about this stage— When the leaders and directors of God's work get back to the basics of intercessory prayer, fasting, and Bible searching, the Holy Spirit takes us all the way back to stage one—multiplying! He gives the ministry a new birth. He recaptures the glory and excitement of early beginnings. Zeal and power flow again.

These apostles chose Stephen and turned the business over to him and his associates. They, in turn, went back to the Upper Room. The sound of praying ministers was heard in the camp. It was contageous; it was like starting all over again. "And the word of God increased; and the number of disciples multiplied in Jerusalem greatly; and a great company of priests were obedient to the faith."

Had the leaders of this movement not returned to seeking God, I shudder to think of the outcome. I can see unsolved problems mounting; an increase in murmuring; mounting bills, perplexity, and despair; rushing around and getting nowhere; getting involved in spectacular ministries without a mandate from God. And I can see frantic staff members standing around on street corners dressed as Santa, hoping someone will fill their little buckets to help pay God's bills!

And it would have all ended up with these disciples dejected, discouraged, going with hat-in-hand to beg the Sanhedrin to bail them out!

But that will never happen to our work—God with us! You are receiving a call from God's throne room to go with me back to our starting place to rededicate ourselves to the principles upon which God founded His work:

Intercessory prayer about every single need.

Faith in God, not in Uncle Sam or the rich!

Praying leaders who shut themselves in the secret

closet and who refuse to come out until God sends the answer.

I'm going back to my first call, to the secret closet, and if you come along, God will send us another Pentecost on our work.

God, make me *your* minister!

13

Cedars in Lebanon And the Trees in Eden

(Ezekiel 31:1-10)

The Assyrians were a great nation planted by great waters, towering over all other nations like a mighty cedar tree. High stature. Exalted greatness.

And the smaller cedars in the garden of God could not compare. All the smaller trees in God's garden (Eden) were not like these big, successful cedars. *No* tree in the garden of God was like unto him (the establishment) in his beauty.

And all the trees in Eden envied him!

There you have in one story all the frustration of those who labor in God's vineyard. They see the great majestic, towering, successful institutions of heathen governments. They have money, prestige, acceptance. And they seem to do it all without God!

And look what we have—with God. In spite of all our faith, our best God-ordained institution cannot compare with the institutions built by Caesars and Napoleons and present-day governments. It awed the disciples. They preached penniless—following a man who had no place to lay His head—and the established forces built temples!

God help us to learn the measurements of God! God is not a building contractor. He is not an empire builder. God is at work molding and making *eternal men*! How many man-made institutions can you look at and say assuredly, "That institution will last forever—it is eternal"? *None!* Just as Jesus predicted, "Not one stone will remain upon another." The glory of one will be the dust of another.

And what about all those insignificant, underfinanced, under-staffed, under-equipped Christian institutions that grow in God's garden? They are eternal. Their buildings mean nothing. Their spirit and life is everything. They are camouflaging a secret that will be revealed the very day Christ returns to the earth.

The next time you are discouraged that a mighty God seems to be sponsoring such weak institutions, take another look and say, "That is an eternal institution. It will never die! That is its greatness. While all its bigger shadows will fade and die, that one will survive—forever!"

The cedars of Lebanon and the trees of Eden will all be brought down to dust—unto the nether parts of the earth (verse 18). But the trees of Eden shall rise again and be flourishing by the waters of the river of life!

14

God, Kill Me

"And it came to pass by the way in the inn, that the Lord met him, and sought to kill him" (Ex. 4:24).

Moses was on his way to gather Israel for departure from Egypt. A great and mighty future lay ahead of this man. And God always meets a man on the way to victory this very same way. There will be a rest stop—a moment of relaxation—and God will appear and have it out with His chosen vessel.

Moses had failed God—in *one* small matter. Circumcision—the sign of separation. God would not invest any future in this man until he destroyed (killed) the old Moses.

Don't look for a mistake in the translation. God was after His man! He was determined to kill and utterly annihilate the last of the stubborn nature that caused a servant to be so obsessed with a vision he could neglect simple acts of obedience.

God is after every true child of His today. Out to meet us in some resting place. Out to destroy the old man—the disobedient, uncircumcised nature.

There is danger in wanting to be free of the eternal

struggle. We want God to end the battle once and for all. We get tired. We no longer choose to resist the devil. We prefer to call it a demon and have it cast out—painlessly, permanently. Or, we choose to seek some kind of divine circumcision with God inflicting the knife. We want the power of sin cut off—finally, once and for all. We want to enter into a life so clean, so holy, we need never sin again. Hallelujah! We all seek that life! But, beware of the dangers.

1. We will be in a fight until God calls off the war. No warrior can sit down, resign, or go AWOL! We fight, we resist, we keep on the armor, we overcome until the very armistice!

2. All *heresy* starts with "a final cure" for the inner struggle! All cults promise the "final blow" against the enemy. Promises of total victory now! No more struggle, no more need to resist! Heaven now!

3. There is only one biblical way to victory over sin, self, and the devil: A vision of the greatness of God, a vision of glorious promises, a revelation that He is greater than any power over us!

15

God Is Great

Moses made the whole world rethink God. His world was full of gods—wooden ones, iron ones, stone ones—male and female. Every natural phenomenon was supposed to be the expression of a different god. Moses, in one short sentence, changed that thinking. *"There is one God—only!"* This concept changed slaves into an organized army of believers.

Amos lived in an age of the wicked, unjust gods of the Greeks—Zeus, an old reprobate who slew anyone who interferred with his love affairs. Amos had a new revelation of God.

"God is just!" He cannot be bribed or bought. He did not discriminate. He would not barter on holiness—giving special indulgences for special favors or sacrifices.

Hosea saw God differently. His wife cheated on him, but he forgave her and took her back. While thinking about it, a great concept entered his mind: *"God is good."* If I can forgive like this, how much more will God forgive my unfaithfulness.

Jesus came to make God personal. His concept was: *"God—our father."* All children equal, all children blessed alike, all heirs, all made one to His honor and glory. There is one God. He is just. He is good. He is *our* Father.

Your young men shall see visions. The vision for the last generation, the apocalyptic age, is: "*God is great!*" The one, just, good, father . . . is great!

"The eyes of your understanding being enlightened: that ye may know what is the hope of his calling, and what the riches of the glory of his inheritance in the saints, and what is the exceeding greatness of his power to usward who believe, according to the working of his mighty power, which he wrought in Christ, when he raised him from the dead, and set him at his own right hand in the heavenly places, far above all principality, and power, and might, and dominion, and every name that is named, not only in this world, but also in that which is to come: and hath put all things under his feet, and gave him to be the head over all things to the church, which is his body, the fulness of him that filleth all in all" (Eph. 1:18-23).

You cannot understand the power of your baptism until you fully understand the power of God. The old man's dream—the young man's vision—is now becoming clear. It is a revelation of God's greatness —a clear revelation that all His power and greatness is available to every child of God.

This generation will close out in a full and final revelation of God's greatness. Prophets dreamed of it—but we now make the discoveries. There will come to this generation an accelerated knowledge of His power. We see through a glass, darkly, but the outlines of His glory now shine through. Eyes are being opened.

"The secret things belong unto the Lord our God: but those things which are revealed belong unto us and to our child for ever" (Deut. 29:29).

16

Greatness

"Neither be ye called masters: for one is your Master, even Christ. But he that is greatest among you shall be your servant. And whosoever shall exalt himself shall be abased; and he that shall humble himself shall be exalted. But woe unto you, scribes and Pharisees, hypocrites! for ye shut up the kingdom of heaven against men: for ye neither go in yourselves, neither suffer ye them that are entering to go in" (Matthew 23:10-13).

We have just lived through the shabbiest decade in all of history. It has been a time of cheating, hypocrisy, addictions, murder, greed, prejudice, hate, and, most of all, spiritual poverty.

I believe we need a new revolution in hearts, homes, and churches. A revolution of *greatness!* This thought comes from Jesus Christ Himself. Christ faced Jewish lawyers, leaders, and Pharisees—and challenged them to greatness. He told them to their face: "Everything you do is for show—you love recognition; you pretend to be holy; you act so great—but you are poor hypocrites." *Then He added:* "He that would be the greatest, must become a servant."

This is one of the most powerful one-verse sermons

Christ ever preached. In one sentence Christ revealed the secret of greatness! No research needed—no hidden meanings—just clear, simple theology: *"Become a servant*—that is the path to greatness!"

Don't let the word "great" turn you off. It doesn't mean *rich, successful,* or *proud.* It stands for: Significant, important, superior, grand, eminent, distinguished, influential, noble.

There is little greatness left in the world today: only a few great people, a few great churches, a few great pastors, a few great young people, because there are very few servants. Everybody is a *master* to himself.

What made the first Pentecostal church great? *Not the preaching!* They were unlearned, ignorant men. I seriously doubt a single great sermon was preached. It was all borrowed theology from the prophets. Paul put them to sleep.

Not the buildings! They worshipped in upper-rooms, beside the rivers, in homes. They were, in fact, cast out of the beautiful synagogues.

Not influence! They had none! They were looked upon as "drunks." They were hounded by city leaders, cast into prisons, despised as the "offscour of the earth." Not one of them could get into the city council—except on a criminal charge.

Not numbers! It began with only 120, and many of them were unknown women! When thousands were converted and their numbers grew, it led to problems innumerable. Their greatness was not in their growth!

They were *great*, the church was *great*, their movement was *great—because they were all servants!* They served their city, their country, their generation! They served one another!

What does Christ really mean—*become a servant?*

Destroy the master complex and humble yourself! Stop playing and indulging—and get to work! "If he finds that servant eating, drinking, . . ." *Stop your spiritual selfishness and feed others first!* "He will make them sit down and will serve the master first." We have become so conscious of our own problems! Little babies fretting over our bottles— while a world goes to hell!

17

We Are Not Born To Serve Only

Why am I here on earth? How can I best please God? What exactly does God want out of me? What can I do to feel satisfied and fulfilled?

Should I spend my life feeding the poor? "The poor you have with you always." She poured incense and perfume on the Master in praise and glory to Him! That is needed—but *not first!*

Should I spend all my time waiting on others? Mary and Martha had to choose! Mary sat and ministered to Christ's spiritual needs! Martha chose wrong—to worry about service to the physical body. This should be done, but not before priorities are right.

Should I build a temple—an institution—to His glory? He said, "Not *one* stone would remain." We are spiritual buildings—to give Him glory in our temple *not* made with hands! Institutions must be built—but not *primary!* They are needed because we fail in individual responsibility!

Shall I go to a foreign mission field and burn out? "If I gave my body to be burned at the stake— and had not charity—*all is vain!*" Think of it!

Missionaries will and must go, but that is our secondary mission. God's glory and praise first! Our main call, purpose, reason for existence is to praise and glorify God and His Son, Jesus.

We bleed for orphans (and we should). We cry over the lost heathen (we should). We canvass the world seeking converts (good). We lose our health raising money to build God memorials to human need (all right). We burn with compassion for the poor, the widowed, the neglected, the impoverished, the downtrodden, the abused, the diseased and broken (wonderful). We scheme, and dream, and plan, and design, and invent ways to do God's work and evangelism, feed and save the world (we must). We are ready to die for Him—burn out—lay our all on any kind of sacrificial altar (amen). We find happiness and fulfillment *only* when we feel we have *done* something for Him—*built* something for Him— or when we can point statistically to some achievement in His name (good). *But* we still have a gnawing inside—an itch that goes unscratched, a deep, unnamed sense of not doing enough. It's a fear of dying without accomplishing some worthwhile task (sadly true). We miss the most simple, clear, easy plan of God for all of us!

HIS PLAN: That every child of heaven spend that life giving glory and praise to God/Christ! God could call down a legion of angels to do His will. He could do all we are doing without us! But—we are predestined to His glory and praise! We are born *not to serve*—but to praise and worship!

18

There's Just Something About That Name

"Howbeit no man spake openly of him for fear of the Jews" (John 7:13).

The Jews' Feast of Tabernacles was in progress. Rumors prevailed everywhere. The Jews sought after Jesus. "Where is He?" the crowds inquired.

His name was bantered around. Some said He was in truth the Son of God. Some said He was an imposter. Others asked, "How could anything good come out of Galilee?" But men took sides.

Yet with all the murmuring about His name—with all the underground discussions—all the seeking after Him to satisfy curiosity—*no man spake openly of Him!* Think of it. An entire city, an entire celebration is totally silent. No one dares publicly mention His name. Why?

For fear of the Jews! Yet there were Jews also who were afraid. And there is a lesson here for us today. Why are presidents, government leaders, world leaders, prominent people so unwilling to mention the name of Jesus openly?

For fear! They are afraid of the consequences.

Few nations have had a leader who unabashedly spoke freely and lovingly of the name of Jesus. How many truly intellectual secular college presidents can you name who are not afraid to openly acknowledge the name and power of Jesus?

There is something about that name! It makes a man decide. Will he openly confess Him on earth or through fear ignore His name?

Give us men who are not afraid to speak His name openly.

19

Not Peter-Not Paul-But Christ

"He answered and said unto them, Well hath Esaias prophesied of you hypocrites, as it is written, This people honoureth me with their lips, but their heart is far from me. Howbeit in vain do they worship me, teaching for doctrines the commandments of men. For laying aside the commandment of God, ye hold the tradition of men, as the washing of pots and cups: and many other such like things ye do. And he said unto them, Full well ye reject the commandment of God, that ye may keep your own traditions" (Mark 7:6-9).

Catholics look to Peter as the rock of their church. Protestants turn to Paul for their message of justification by faith. Peter and Paul followers make poor Christ followers.

It's time for an honest look at the Charismatic Movement, both in the Catholic and Protestant circles. On the surface it would appear a new church is springing up—that Protestants and Catholics are getting closer and closer and that the theology gap is closing and a true Holy Ghost ecumenical movement has come.

Catholics are becoming Pentecostals. Pentecostals and other Protestants are worshipping together. A spiritual revival is spreading everywhere.

But there are some very serious cracks developing in the unity wall. The "togetherness gate" is swinging back and forth on rusty hinges. Catholic charismatics are beginning to realize how addicted to Peter they have become. The Holy Father and the mother church and all the traditions are still very much a part of every pronouncement.

We are not united by tongues but by the mutual *love for Christ* prompted by the Holy Ghost.

It is not charisma—but Christ! Not Peter, not Paul —but Christ!

Peter would denounce every tongue-talking Bishop who declared: "We need Peter!"

Paul would cry out against every Protestant who preached Paul and not Christ!

Speaking in tongues is not a badge of holiness, a secret pass into God's inner sanctum, a kind of rubber stamp of heaven that always reads, "Approved."

Can Catholics and Protestants worship together? Can they put aside unscriptural traditions on both sides and meet at the foot of the cross? Can the Holy Spirit raise up a truly ecumenical church in which only God's Holy Word is the foundation of all teaching and practice?

Yes! But probably not until all the traditionalists die in the wilderness. Not until the umprejudiced young come of age!

Not until Christ is first! Not until we see the church as invisible—in Him alone. Not until the pope, the bishop, the vicar, the superintendent, the pastor is seen in his scriptural position as God's servant under Christ's yoke!

Not until Peter decreases and Christ increases! Not until Paul is hidden behind the glory of the cross. Not until He is fully recognized as Head of the church. Not until the cross overshadows the upper room.

20

How to Understand Parents

Teenagers of today keep screaming about their need to be understood. Most of them seem convinced their parents are not really capable of directing them the way they want to be directed. The number one complaint I hear from kids against parents is always, "My parents just don't understand me at all!"

If I am to believe most teenagers, and the experts who echo and reinforce their complaints, I would have to believe parents are the most stupid, bungling, incompetents on earth. To hear them tell it, parents must stay awake all night scheming of ways to make life miserable for their kids. Parents, they say, don't understand fashions, friends, loafing around, long hair, heavy music, or any of the other "cool" things that make up much of teenage activity.

Hogwash! In the first place, I believe most parents try to be understanding. The mother who warns her daughter that her wild boyfriend is "just a creep" is usually right. He usually is a creep, and that "misunderstanding" mother, who puts her foot down, is probably saving the girl's life. Yet, mother is supposed to understand her girl's "need" to associate with a no-good, disreputable boy!

Secondly, I doubt if any parent can understand a teenager fully. That teenage mind is changing gears every two or three minutes. It is a moody way of life, riding the waves of fleeting and very fickle emotions. While parents are still "grieving" over a certain problem, that teenager goes merrily on the way, having forgotten it completely, or having substituted another "life and death" problem.

If we're going to spend so much time demanding understanding, I want in on the act, too. I'm a parent—I want to be understood, too. Why not demand that kids swallow a big dose of their own medicine?

I love my children dearly, and I love all teenagers. But now, when one comes up to me and complains, "My parents don't understand me," I immediately reply, "But have you tried to understand them?"

Honestly now, teenager, if you want to be understood, you must learn to understand your parents first. And I have some very practical suggestions on just how to accomplish that. As a parent, I know of at least eight ways kids can understand dads and moms.

1. *Think of your parents as much as you think of yourself!*

"Maturity begins to grow when your concern for others outweighs your concern for self."

To many teenagers are selfish about love and understanding. They want it all one way, in *their* direction. A high regard and respect for parents is the first essential in a good relationship. Jesus knew He was sent from the Father above, yet He honored His earthly father and mother with total respect and reverence.

2. *Try some humility!*

"Love is learning how to say, I'm sorry."

Parents respond to honest humility. There is not a problem between kids and parents that cannot be solved when there is a genuine willingness to admit: "I was wrong; forgive me!"

3. *Quit blaming them for all your personal problems!*

"Love looks beyond all faults and sees the need."

Parents seem to be blamed for everything. Homosexuality is blamed on a "weak" father or an "overbearing" mother. Everyone wants to pass the buck—but it stops with the parents. Sure, parents are to blame often, but not always. They have a need to know you carry no grudges against them for things that go wrong in your life.

4. *Be patient with them!*

"Patience is the ability to trust that others will eventually do the job as well as you."

Parents are human—terribly human—and practical. There is not an angel among them, and the sooner you understand that, the sooner you will understand them. You want them to give you a chance. Why not give them the same chance? Don't put parents on some dreamy pedestal, and don't expect miracles from them. Treat them like humans who need a margin for error.

5. *Accept them "As Is"!*

"Love covers a multitude of sins."

Quit star gazing. Let your parents be just "plain folks." If Dad drinks, or if Mother screams and curses, pray for them. But never give up on them. Never put them down or make them feel like failures as parents. You allow yourself room for improvement. Can't you allow them time to do better, also? Parents know when they are setting a poor example, and your trust in them in spite of their weaknesses can often bring them back to reality.

6. *Don't pity yourself!*

"Perfect love casteth out all fear."

Pity is based on fear, and parents can be made to feel very small by teenagers who use it as a weapon or excuse. If you cannot honestly face up to conditions as they really are, you will wallow around in self-pity—and that can affect parents deeply. They can sense when you are ashamed of them, the way they dress or act, the job Dad has, the home they provide—or their inability to give you all the desires of your heart! Grow up—and get down off the "miff" tree.

7. *Don't be gullible!*

"Love looks beyond what a person is and believes in what he can be."

Never let an "expert" prejudice you against your parents. Most of what is written about them consists of half-truths and unproven philosophies. Never take sides. Love Dad and Mother with the same fervor and zeal. Forget all the big talk about "generation gaps" and parental neglect. If there is a gap between you and your parents, you have allowed it to develop, and it's your responsibility to do something about it, too! If left alone, you and your parents should be able to work it out. It's always a third party who causes the trouble.

8. *Be honest with parents!*

"Love is not something you talk about—It's something you do."

If you will quit bluffing your parents—if you will quit pretending and playing games—things will change quickly. Parents know you better than you think they do. Let them see the real you, not just a robot that goes around shooting off negative vibrations. Honestly now, do you clean your room? Help with household chores? Eat right? Run with the right crowd? Obey the basic family rules? Should you? You bet you should! Be honest about it! Isn't it true most of your problems can be traced right back to a little cheating somewhere on your part? Parents respond to honesty like flowers respond to rain. Try it!

The Bible sums it all up in one powerful commandment: "Love your father and mother that your days may be long on the earth" (Eph. 6:2, 3).

21

Please Do As I Do

Let me talk about the old cliche you often hear quoted: "Don't look at me. Get your eyes off men. Don't do as I do. Keep your eyes only on Jesus."

This is a cop-out. Paul the apostle set the record straight when he said, "Look at me and follow my example—The things you see in me—do" (I Tim. 1:16).

This man of God was not afraid of falling or being a stumbling block to others. In fact, Paul boasted that he was a "pattern."

When a child of God is living in harmony with the Word and the Spirit, he should not be afraid to let the whole world look to him, and he should not be afraid to encourage others to do just as he does.

The Christian is not to fear the concept of other Christians trying to emulate their lives. When the life we live is Christlike, we should want the whole world to live likewise. We must never limit the exemplifying power of Christ Jesus in the believer. If God sees fit to allow you to go through deep waters and tests you to the limit, it is only to bring you out victoriously so that *all the more* you will be an example for others to follow.

Don't be afraid of being an example for others. Don't cringe under the gaze of eyes upon you. Don't hide behind a mask of phony humility when a young Christian tells you, "I want to be just like you." Like Paul, you probably have many weaknesses and perhaps even a thorn in your flesh. But like him, you can be a pattern for others by fully trusting in the grace of Jesus Christ that flows through your life.

Furthermore, Paul said, "You are all partakers of my grace" (Phil. 1:7). To every convert, Paul said, "I have you in my heart . . . you are all partakers of my grace" (Phil. 1:7). In actuality, he told them, "You would never have found grace except through me. God blessed me and gave me grace, and you have been partakers of my grace."

Every man, woman, and child of God has a certain "grace." It is a supernatural gift from God and can be imparted to others. Many times I have laid hands upon the head of some youngster whom I know God is about to bless, and I have prayed, "Lord, take of the spirit you have placed on me and place it on this youngster."

You have a grace about you whether you know it or not. It has nothing to do with your personality, but instead represents the way in which the Holy Spirit works in your life. It is a personal "light" the Holy Spirit ignites in each believer, and God commands that we allow it to shine forth.

God promised to give us "sufficient grace." That actually means enough to give to others. This "marvelous grace of Jesus" can be transmitted to others, and it has about it a beautiful contagious reaction. What you share always comes back many fold.

Paul, while in prison, boasted to the whole world, "The confirmation of God upon my ministry is found in all those who partook of my grace" (Phil. 1:7). This prisoner of Christ had a very special grace. And what is this special grace we all share with the apostle? It is a forgiving spirit that reaches out to reconcile everything to God.

God, give us Christians who have so much confidence in the grace of Christ in their lives, they can face the whole world and say, "Do as I do—speak as I speak—follow my example." If we cannot be "patterns" for our master builder, then we must consign ourselves as rejects with no place in the construction of God's holy Kingdom.

Excerpts From Letters

Gossip

Dear Mr. Wilkerson:

In your latest "Report" there is an article about gossip. It made me realize all the more how badly gossip sneaks up on us and invades every corner of our lives.

About a year ago I received a note in the mail from one of the sponsors of a singing group I was in. She was commending me because I didn't gossip like the other girls in our group did. I was flattered, but even so, I wasn't the type to get a swelled head. It got me to thinking though. I never really noticed it before, but after that I was only too painfully aware of how much I did gossip, and it was horrible.

J.C.
Hannibal, Missouri

Dear Mr. Wilkerson:

Thank you for your straightforward approach to the crooked-backward approach called gossip.

Amen to what you have written. I'm rebuked at, "I'm only telling you this as a prayer request." I am guilty and am confessing my fault before my Lord.

J.C.
Fairbanks, Alaska

Dear Mr. Wilkerson:

Upon reading your article, "Speaking Out About Gossip," I fully agree with your attitude toward it. My wife and I fell victim to it a few years ago. There were people saying things that were not true about us. Many times I challenged the persons to see me and tell me what they were saying. As of this day no one has shown up. The thing that hurts most is the fact that the people involved are supposedly "strict" members of Christ's body. How true is the book of James in the third chapter which says, "The tongue can no man tame," and that it is "unruly, evil, full of deadly poison."

L.E.B.
Pella, Iowa

Dear Mr. Wilkerson:

This is in response to your article on gossip. I could not agree with you more. So this letter is not only one to say how great your article is but also a confession. I am an ordained minister. I went to a junior college for two years and presently I am a ministerial student at Stamford University. But what I'm trying to say is I am guilty of all the very things you said. And, after reading this column on gossip, I'm going to turn it over to God in prayer and ask for His help in watching my tongue. Would you please pray for me?

B.B.
Birmingham, Alabama

Dear Mr. Wilkerson:

This letter comes in response to your article on gossip. In the letter accompanying the report you invited us to join in your nation-wide crusade to stop gossip. I want you to know that I am behind you 100% in this effort.

Before I go any further, let me confess that I too have been a tool in Satan's hand, used as he attempted to strike out at various ministries. I am only 19 years old, but I have been a Christian for 13 of those years. I am just beginning to realize the damage that can be caused by gossip under the guise of prayerful concern. I have decided to keep my mouth shut, except to defend men and women of God who are the objects of slanderous talk.

I had often wondered why men and women of God who had apparently found the answers for themselves would not speak out when there were so many Christians with so much potential just waiting to find the answers themselves. May God bless you as you continue to speak out as the Spirit leads.

D.A.
Baton Rouge, Louisiana

Dear Mr. Wilkerson:

Just the other day I was working with a few of my girlfriends (mostly Christian) and we were talking about people who we thought needed prayer. But then we ended up talking about their faults and their friends and so on and so on.... I used to think that it really wasn't *gossiping*, just concern. Or that it was okay since it was true.

Well, that same day I came home and found the newsletter so I opened it up, looked at the pictures, and started to put it down when the word "gossip" caught my attention. So I read the article and it was like God speaking to me.

J.B.
Yakima, Washington

Dear Mr. Wilkerson:

I completely agree with what you said in your report about gossip. This subject has really bugged me for a long time because I know it has helped to kill my church. I am a senior in high school, and I belong to a small church. For about four years there has been gossip circulating in our church, and it has been snowballing and has gotten worse each year. Many times I and my family have spread gossip also and have many times been hurt by it.

During the summer of 1971 I received the baptism of the Holy Spirit in Nashville and started living for Christ. Gossip is a vicious thing and I have still found myself caught up in it some times. But now when I hear it, it cuts like a dagger, so I try to stay clear and stop as much gossip as I can.

Please be in prayer for my church as it is a victim of the powers of gossip and is sinking quickly.

N.S.
Beltsville, Maryland

Dear Mr. Wilkerson:

Thank you so much for your article "Speaking Out About Gossip." I must confess it really hit home. As you wrote, I used to tell people gossip "so they could pray about it." I thank you, and praise the Lord, that I can help in the fight against gossip by stopping gossip with myself. I will pass on your article, in love and concern, so others may gain from it. This week I'm going back to college in Bowling Green, Ohio. Even as a member of "Navigators," a Christian group, it's easy to get caught up in idle gossip. Through the power of the Holy Spirit, I hope to gain victory over this sin.

Thank you again. I agree with you wholeheartedly.

D.O.
Bowling Green, Ohio

Dear Mr. Wilkerson:

I appreciate your article entitled "Speaking Out Against Gossip." The day I got it in the mail and looked at the title, God began to deal with me. In fact, I didn't even read it, but the title convicted me. I read it a day later.

I realize that I, too, have been an unwitted Christian young person. I have, in the same methods as you, been spreading gossip when I should have kept my mouth shut.

I guess God has really been trying to teach me this all along but it took your article to bring it into focus for me.

R.Y.
Rocky Ford, Colorado

Dear David:

This is in reply to the gossip letter that you sent out. You asked for replies and for once I thought I'd write.

Somehow all the "Cross and the Switchblade" magazines, whether they be things like "I'm Fed Up" or "The Forgotten Teenager," will always make me cry. This was no exception. I found myself in the teaching just like you did. Many people I know, including myself, have really just ruined some people in our community. Thank you so much for listening to the Lord and then telling everybody about it. There's another part of my life that Satan has just lost. I'll have no part of spreading gossip anymore.

C.S.
Niagara Falls, New York

Dear Brother Wilkerson:

I have just read your outstanding article on gossip out of your report.

My husband and I are presently living with my sister here on the campus of a Bible college. We came from Idaho seven weeks ago with broken hearts —and shattered plans due to vicious gossip of our brethren in Idaho. My husband is an ordained minister. (In fact, I was a classmate of yours in 1949-1953.)

In our pastorate in Idaho, we received 100% support for three years—until Satan leveled a sudden campaign of *lies* and gossip against us. We finally resigned our church and tried to obtain another pastorate, but we found the gossip had preceded us—so we were never voted in.

We sought other employment, but the first week on the job my husband was confronted with these words from his employer, "Mr. ——, a former church member of yours, came in today and asked me if I knew I had hired an embezzler and an adulterer." We tried to ride out the storm, trusting God to work it "together for good."

In the weeks that followed we received vicious, anonymous phone calls, asking, among other things, if "my husband had raped any little girls lately"— and threats that our home would be burned, and that our small son was going to be killed. Our garage, which was 2 feet from our house, was one night soaked with gasoline and about 2:30 a.m. last November 24 (Thanksgiving night), we awoke to an exploding fire which had totally consumed our garage. Only quick response from the fire department saved our home. One month later we received another phone call saying, "This time we won't make a mistake. Your home will burn."

The gossip concerned our youth leader whose husband was not a Christian—and who had loyally stood by us. There was not one shred of truth to the gossip.

I, the wife, would swear by the integrity of my husband and our accused youth leader.

Eventually the home of the youth leader was broken by the suspicions which had been planted in the mind of her husband. In court last February when the evidence against my husband was presented (in their divorce case), the judge refused to even consider it because it was all so ridiculous, and obviously trumped up.

Our district brethren withdrew from us. Our presbyter refused to recommend us even for fill-in.

In the past two years my husband suffered two heart attacks, entering hospitals a total of seven times (the first time for 30 days).

The hospital, doctor, and druggist bills became insurmountable. We lost our home.

In desperation last July my husband came to California to try to find either a pastorate or a job. He found a good job and brought me, his wife, and our smallest daughter here to live with my sister. Our other two children, a senior and sophomore, are yet in Idaho with my parents until we are permanently located.

But because of the financial drain, we are presently filing for bankruptcy through which we will probably lose most of our furniture accumulated the past 17 years of our marriage.

Now what? We live from day to day, praising God that He is sovereign, and that He gave us strength through it all—and for the wonderful friends who have stood by us, for healing my husband, for doing a deep work in our lives through it all.

We have endured rejection from the "world" since our conversion—but it doesn't even compare with the hurt which came from the *hatred* and rejection of our deacons, fellow ministers, and lifelong friends.

I pray God will use you to throw confusion into this vicious tool of Satan's of gossip, and stop this flood of evil which may eventually be leveled against every ministry.

R.S.
Santa Cruz, California

Tongues

Dear David:

This summer I'm working as a Youth Director and Minister of Music in a church here. I was brought up in a very spiritual home. And since going off to school I have plunged into deeper spiritual things. The Lord blessed me with the gift of tongues.

I really appreciate your honesty. I respect a man more, even if I don't always agree with him, if I know he's being open and honest.

Our fellowship at school was a real close-knit group of kids some of whom spoke in tongues and some who didn't. But it didn't make any difference. We were of all denominations and backgrounds, but that didn't interfere with our love for Jesus and each other.

I wish more people had this open-minded approach that you have. I hate to see the divisive aspect involved with tongues, but to me it's not tongues but people who are divisive.

B.B.
Opp, Alabama

Dear Mr. Wilkerson:

I wanted to acknowledge your January news-letter. Keep at it, preacher! Sure, you've stepped on a few toes, maybe. But everything you have said the last 6 months has been said lovingly and kindly.

I particularly enjoyed your essay on tongues. It was "where I am."

I pray daily in tongues but it is not for me to judge another man's gifts.

Sure, I disagree with some of the things you say. Our Lord didn't say we always have to *agree* with one another; He said we always have to *love* one another. So keep it up and God bless you. I pray for you and your work daily.

F.E.
Florence, Alabama

Dear Brother Wilkerson:

As an evangelist traveling across the country, I have encountered many of the issues you talked about in "Speaking Out." I have found that the non-Pentecostals want to claim you until they find out you speak in tongues. The Pentecostals want to claim you until you say you can receive the baptism without speaking in tongues. I usually reply, "Why not just do as Jesus did?" He told them to be saved, baptized and filled and go on! If a person wants me to pray for him to receive the Holy Spirit but says he doesn't want those tongues, you bet I pray with him. God will reveal that tongues are real and for today when he is ready for this.

I have never seen His Word fail yet. I know I never shall.

C.P.
Burleson, Texas

Dear David:

In my four years in high school, I was fortunate to be surrounded by good biblical teaching and a neat group of Christians. As I grew up in my understanding of the Word, I reached the conclusion that tongues were not a criterion of spiritual maturity, and that baptism of the Holy Spirit today meant being controlled and filled by/with Him. So I became critical of the churches and organizations who stressed tongues so much. I became especially opposed to tongues, as I heard many Pentecostals in our area saying that you could be a Christian only if you spoke in tongues. That was biblically wrong and, I felt, destructive. Also, I saw many people in our school become involved in a highly emotional tongues movement that didn't stress the Word at all, and many fell away as the emotions wore off. Seeing these things, I adopted a very critical attitude toward the tongues movement.

However, someone wisely pointed out to me that we can realize that as groups of Christians, organizations, and demonstrations may have weaknesses and sin, we can forgive each other because the Lord has forgiven us. God's just been putting it on my heart to be cleansed of a critical attitude toward the Pentecostal believers. I believe the Lord gives different gifts to all, and that they are to be used not for ourselves but to edify the body. But, too, I see that as a body, small differences or even large doctrinal differences are not to divide us.

I wanted to let you know what the Lord has done in my heart in my attitudes toward yours and other ministries. We can disagree on issues, but our common bond should continue to be our belief in Christ and our love for each other.

I especially appreciate the stand you've been taking recently in your newletters. I realize the difficulty of taking a stand, perhaps especially in Christian circles, where tolerance runs short and love may be lacking.

I am excited to realize the unity we have in Christ!

S.B.
San Jose, California

Dear Mr. Wilkerson:

I have been distressed at the way the body of Christ has been torn to pieces by anti-charismatic people who insist that speaking in tongues is of the enemy and by charismatic people who insist that without this manifestation a person cannot be Spirit-filled. The mediating position which you espouse so effectively in this paper is certainly to be an evidence of the work of the Spirit in healing the terrible divisions among us.

J.R.M.
Columbia, South Carolina

Demons

Dear David:

Your newsletter has laid unopened on my table since it came four days ago. This afternoon the Lord led me to open it. The article on demons was meant for my heart.

Just recently I have been exposed to so much "new" theology, I have begun to wonder where I've been all these years. Casting out demons and healing have shaken me a little. Statements like, "All sickness is of the devil and can be cured by casting out the demon" have not rung true to me, but I didn't know Bible teachings on it so I have said nothing.

All of this is to thank you for your article and let you know what an answer to prayer it has been to me.

J.J.
Valdosta, Georgia

Dear Brother Wilkerson:

I just want to let you know that I think you should

keep "speaking out." I don't believe the Lord wants people supporting your work only as long as you agree with them (or vice versa) or because of your influence. There are certain areas that I don't agree with you on, but that is not the basis of our oneness in Christ Jesus.

I basically agree with you concerning demons. I believe the only way a Christian can have demon trouble is by open invitation (disobedience to God in partaking in occult practices or heretical religions). Otherwise I am completely repulsed by the idea of Christians who love the Lord being inhabited by demons. Just last night I witnessed a young Christian torturously "delivered" by some well-meaning businessmen of everything imaginable, including such things as lust, pride, anger, hate, wrath, asthma, influenza, and about a dozen other things. Apparently they were satisfied because each "demon" came out with vomiting, gagging, and screaming.

This is disgraceful. I come from a fundamental, independent church where the work of the Holy Spirit is misunderstood because of things like this. How much more profitable it would have been to have spent three hours encouraging that fellow, praying with him, sharing Scripture with him to get him rooted and grounded and settled in the hope that he has in Christ.

I know that deliverance ministry apart from the Word of God is extremely dangerous. I underwent "deliverance" last year to get rid of a little problem in my personal life, and when the problem came back, my faith was almost shattered. But through the Scriptures I could see that my problem was laziness and indifference which was keeping me from having victory.

Gradually I could praise the Lord again and rejoice in the promises of the Bible. (I really cling to Ephesians 2 and Colossians 1 when people try to pry out some "demons.") I do believe in demons, but I praise God I don't have to worry about them. According to Scripture, my biggest hassle is ME. If I can daily reckon myself dead to sin and alive to righteousness, then that's victory and it's up to me. I'm free in Christ, not subject to demonic bondage or to people who worry about demons.

I have also come to be careful of people who, every time they see "deliver" in the Bible, connect it with deliverance from demons. It has been 3 years since my spiritual baptism, and I can truly say that I have been (and am being) delivered from fear, nervousness, self-condemnation and a lot of other negative things which the Lord wanted to replace with His joy and peace.

Another thing I don't understand is why people insist that demons "name themselves" before they are cast out. Didn't Jesus tell them to be silent? I have seen people's fellowship destroyed because somebody found out what kind of "demon" so-and-so had, and pretty soon everybody knew, and it might not have been something to be publicly shared. A friend of mine wasn't getting victory over masturbation, and it wasn't long till practically every charismatic in the area was saying, "Did you hear what kind of demon *he* has?" Between the weird teaching on demons and the gossip, the poor guy could only feel at home fellowshipping with the religious liberals. Fortunately, today the whole thing has cleared up, and he is in the U.S. Navy living victoriously for the Lord.

Well, I guess I have "spoken out." I will continue to pray for and support your ministry.

B.S.
Indiana, Pennsylvania

Dear Brother Wilkerson:

I too have encountered many problems in the demonic teaching area. If I am reading you right, I believe you agree with me that a Spirit-filled Christian cannot be possessed but may be oppressed by Satan. Am I correct in assuming this? I have a very dear friend (a minister) who had teaching in this area and had many things cast off and came to me with such a spirit of fear I had to pray for him myself. There is some truth there but much error, I feel, and of course the devil is running with it fast.

I attended some meetings in California four years ago, and being new in the Word I was very upset at the much glorification the devil was getting and the little God was getting. I began to pray for this minister then. In the past year, however, I have heard him say himself that he would give anything to recall all the tapes he made before as they do not give enough praise to Jesus. Many others have been praying with me for him, and I truly believe we are now seeing the fruits of our prayers.

C.P.
Burleson, Texas

Dear Brother Wilkerson:

The section of your letter on demonology is right-on. It has troubled us greatly to see brethren delivering people with techniques learned only from other men's experiences. We have been learning here that Satan will play whatever games with God's people they want to play, bringing whatever physical manifestations they expect, out of the trembling soul on whom they lay their hands. Satan's power over men is gained through fear (Hebrews 2:14, 15). God's people are reading the "deliverance" polemics, and fear is being ministered to them. They are sitting in "deliverance" meetings trembling, thinking: "What if I have a demon I don't know about?" Demon obsession is actually being ministered to God's people through this fear that enters their hearts.

We praise God by telling about His wondrous works, by speaking out of His mighty power. We praise Satan in the same way. God's power is loosed through praise. Satan's power is also loosed this way. We must get back to the Word of God to define what Satan is doing today. We must be able to say to Satan: "God says . . ." rather than, "I read in this or that book."

C.M.
Eau Claire, Wisconsin

Money Raising

Dear Reverend Wilkerson:

The first thing I want to say is amen to your last publication. You certainly didn't lose my support by what you said about money raising. I agreed with you! And I want you to know I wouldn't support you with my prayers and contributions if I didn't have complete trust and faith in your work. I have been tempted many times to send you my tithes. Maybe that would be wrong, I don't know. But in my opinion, you use my money more for the Lord's work than my church does. My contributions aren't much I know 'cause I'm still in high school and I don't have a job, but I do believe with all my heart that the money I do send helps a small bit in bringing people to the Jesus I personally know. I don't begrudge one cent I send you. And I can say the Lord has blessed me. Anyone who stops supporting you because of what you said is better off. Jesus is not going to love the person who begrudges money he gives to the Lord no matter how much is given.

As long as your work is lifting up Jesus, you will

receive the prayers and money you need to continue His work. I give cheerfully because I believe your work is inspired and led by Jesus Christ.

K.G.
Johnson City, Tennessee

The Forgotten Housewife

Dear Mr. Wilkerson:

Several years ago I was a frustrated, forgotten housewife, but as I rededicated my life to Jesus, I surrendered my all: myself, my home, and my family. I gave all I had but God outgives me every time. This is not a letter about me, but about God's giving.

After my surrender I tried and tried to follow Christ with all of me. I was able to guide my children to His Word in church and church school. He promised those who thirst shall be filled. Oh! to claim His promises. God made it possible for me to attend both nights of your crusade here in Houston, Texas, in September.

I didn't have a baby sitter so I took my two small children (5 and 6 years old) the first night along with two women who walk in the Spirit. The second night I took my two small children again and also my teenage daughter (16). I instructed the teen-ager if the Holy Spirit moved her that I would be waiting. We sat near the front and the two girls (age 6 and 16) sat two rows ahead of me.

When you made the altar call the Holy Spirit moved Virginia (16) and she went forward. Emily (6) came back to where I was sitting holding her sleeping brother and asked me if she could go forward. I talked to her softly and reminded her that she had given her heart to Christ, but if she wanted to do it again she could do it right in her seat and Jesus would certainly come in. Then the thought reminded me of the scripture—Do not stand in the way of the little ones. If you do, it would be better to have a millstone around your neck and be cast into the sea. That was strong so I immediately asked for forgiveness and complete guidance. Jesus granted both. This child, who is normally obedient, stood straight up in front of me and said, "Mother, something is buzzing all around inside of me. Can I go up there?" Yes, yes, yes. I thanked God and waited until the "afterglow" service was over. As we walked to the parking lot, I asked Virginia what made her go forward, and she said she wanted to give 100%.

I pray for all our Lutherans to know this true Jesus. The best is yet to come.

E.G.
Houston, Texas

The New Church

Dear David Wilkerson:

Thank you so much for speaking out for "the new church." My parents are very much against me attending a county youth group. The main reason is that it's held in the home of a couple of a different religion than my parents. I feel that your article has given them a few of the reasons I like to attend. My parents also are opposed to my participation in our youth group's services as they feel it's a "big show." I enjoy worshiping Christ through singing and witnessing, but they oppose it because it involves kids of "all different religions," and they feel that it's off balance. My explanations don't seem to count. They think that the influence will persuade me to leave my home church and join this one to which the sponsoring couple belongs. They know of one person that has done this very thing. Why do they feel this way?

Thanks for listening. It feels better to get it out in the open.

M.M.
Cedar Point, Kansas

Dear David:

I just received another copy of your magazine and am impressed with your article on "The New Church." I like especially the sentence, "Let's go hand-in-hand into the world and witness about Christ!"

I've been teaching in Catholic schools for the past 20 years. This past week our faculty has been quite disturbed over division in the parish caused by the pastors. We pray that these difficulties will be resolved in a Christian way. If only your words would be realized to a greater extent in today's world!

M.G.
Milwaukee, Wisconsin